D1101593

Aberdeenshire
...NCIL
...rie

RIO

My Decade as a RED

Bonnier
BOOKS

First published in Great Britain by
Bonnier Books
Appledram Barns
Birdham Road
Chichester PO20 7EQ, UK

Publishing Manager: Perminder Mann
Consulting Editor: Tom Watt
Project Editors: Richard Johnson and Paul Stephens
Editor: Simon Holland
Design Manager: Kathryn Morgan
Design: Mike Buckley & Dynamo Design Limited

ISBN 978-1-905825-58-5

A CIP catalogue record for this book is available
from the British Library.

Printed in the United Kingdom by
Butler Tanner & Dennis Ltd.

Colour reproduction by Aylesbury Studios Ltd.

1 3 5 7 9 8 6 4 2

www.bonnierbooks.co.uk

Bonnier Books is an imprint of
the Bonnier Publishing Group
www.bonnierpublishing.co.uk

RIO

My Decade as a RED

TAKE YOUR
RIO RED DECADE
EXPERIENCE BEYOND
THE PRINTED PAGE

Access exclusive videos using the *Rio Red Decade* app. Download the free app from iTunes or Google Play, point your device at the pages that display the special icon (shown left), and the videos will be revealed on screen. Here you will get the chance to meet my team-mates and friends to see what they have to say about me.

The *Rio Red Decade* app requires an internet connection to be downloaded, and can be used on iPhone, iPad or Android devices. For direct links to download the app and further information, visit www.bonnierbooks.co.uk/rioreddecadeapp

This app is compatible with iPhone 3GS, iPhone 4, iPhone 4S, iPhone 5, iPad 2 Wi-Fi, iPad 2 Wi-Fi + 3G, iPad (3rd generation), iPad Wi-Fi + 4G, iPad (4th generation), iPad Wi-Fi + Cellular (4th generation), iPad mini and iPad mini Wi-Fi + Cellular. Requires iOS 4.3 or later. For Android devices, the app is compatible with Android version 4.0 and above.

 Scan this page to hear Rio introduce *Rio My Decade as a Red*

"He's just a top, top player. Someone who's probably been the best player in his position for the last ten years."

Ryan Giggs

CONTENTS

THE GAFFER

A foreword by
SIR ALEX FERGUSON

Manchester United has been in existence for more than 130 years, and in that time the club has been privileged to have enjoyed the services of some of the finest players ever to kick a football. Most United supporters would be able to reel off the names of the true greats who have helped to bring fame, triumph and success to one of the world's most famous sporting institutions. Invariably, the names that first spring to mind are those of the forwards and strikers who grab the headlines with their match-winning exploits in front of goal. Denis Law, George Best, Eric Cantona, Cristiano Ronaldo, Jack Rowley, Robin van Persie – to name but a few – all slot neatly into that category. Those are the players who receive most of the plaudits, and some would say rightly so, but football is a game of 11-a-side and it's a fact that every player is equally important. Goalkeepers, defenders, midfielders and forwards couldn't function without the efforts of the other departments, and Manchester United has had its fair share of the best in all those sections of the team. Over the years, the club has been blessed by a string of terrific central defenders, who provided the bedrock on which some of the trophy-winning sides were built. Charlie Roberts was a stalwart of the first title-winning team in the years before the First World War, while Frank Barson was a no-nonsense operator in the 1920s.

Sir Matt Busby's first great side had Allenby Chilton and in later years Bill Foulkes converted from full-back to become a highly respected centre-half. More recently, and during my time as the club's manager, United have had some top-bracket central defenders. Steve Bruce, Gary Pallister, Jaap Stam, Nemanja Vidic and, one of the finest of all, Rio Ferdinand. Times were when a central defender's main purpose was to provide a strong, rugged and intimidating barrier. That, of course, is still the case, but in more recent years they have become footballers in their own right and many modern-day central defenders could easily convert to play in midfield or attack. Rio Ferdinand is definitely one of those as he possesses fabulous technical ability, brilliant ball control and is a magnificent reader of the game.

As a youngster, at West Ham's famed academy, he was always earmarked to make it all the way to the top. After having established himself in the West Ham first team it was only a matter of time before other clubs would begin to take a more serious interest in his talents, and it was no real surprise when he was transferred to Leeds United for a (then) record fee. He had already played for England and was fast becoming one of the hottest defensive properties in the game. I'm happy to say that for slightly more than two years we negotiated his move across the Pennines to Old Trafford in exchange for another extremely large cheque. It was another of those occasions when lots of people questioned our decision to splash such an enormous amount of money, but we knew exactly what we were doing. The seasons since have proved conclusively that we were right to raid the bank. Rio Ferdinand stands shoulder-to-shoulder with all of Manchester United's great central defenders, and he can rightly claim a place in the Manchester United 'Hall of Fame'. His performances have been remarkably consistent and inspiring during his career with us, and I'm delighted for the club that he recently signed an extension to his contract. Rio richly deserves the opportunity to celebrate his many splendid years at Old Trafford, with our fans, and I wish him well both for his testimonial and for the future.

THE EARLY YEARS

1996/2002

Ten years old, South London's biggest Maradona fan and wearing borrowed Hi-Tec Strikers that were two sizes too big for me: my first proper game for Bloomfield Athletic. My cousin Ben played for them, my uncle Dave coached, and that was it for me. I fell in love with football. I'd kicked a ball around on our estate, the Friary in Peckham, since I could walk. But this was the real thing: the start of a professional footballer's story.

West Ham	Games	(Subs)	Goals	Yellow	Red
(1996–2000)	154	(6)	2	16	0
Honours: UEFA Intertoto Cup winner (1999)					

Bournemouth	Games	(Subs)	Goals	Yellow	Red
(1997, on loan)	11	(0)	0	0	0

Leeds United	Games	(Subs)	Goals	Yellow	Red
(2000–2002)	73	(0)	3	3	0
Honours: PFA Team of the Year (2001/02)					

It was actually Frank Lampard's dad who got me into West Ham in the first place. I can still remember a couple of times when Frank Senior came to scout me in under-14 games and Frank came along to watch, too. Frank was a year older than me but we became good mates. We played for the reserves together – we used to wait around for the coach to take us off to games and it was always me and Frank playing pool. And later we ended up rooming together: a great friendship.

When I was playing for West Ham's youth teams, if we went behind in a game they'd often put me up front hoping I'd get a goal. And then – if I did – I'd go straight back to playing in defence. It was like something from the pages of Roy of the Rovers. I made my first team debut for West Ham on May 5 1996, subbed on for the last five minutes at home to Sheffield Wednesday.

After that Euro '96 summer, I went out on loan to Bournemouth. By the beginning of February 1997, though, I was back at West Ham and gaffer Harry Redknapp brought me on at half-time – as a striker – away to Blackburn Rovers. Twenty minutes later, I scored my first senior goal: a volley from 15 yards out. Yet more Roy of the Rovers stuff! By the following season I was playing every week alongside the likes of Eyal Berkovic, John Hartson, Frank Lampard and Trevor Sinclair. I couldn't believe it when the supporters voted me Hammer of the Year.

"Harry suggested going out on loan to Bournemouth in late 1996 and it was the making of me. I came back to Upton Park ready – no, desperate – for first team football."

Three Hammers become Three Lions (above);
shades of 1966.

It's 15 November 1997, England versus Cameroon at Wembley. And I'm playing for my country for the first time. When Gareth Southgate got injured, just before half-time, Glenn Hoddle put me on alongside Sol Campbell. This was the stuff of childhood dreams: the crowd chanting "Rio! Rio!" My family were all there in the crowd. And five minutes later, thanks to Paul Scholes and Robbie Fowler, we were 2–0 up. I could even have made it three in the second half, but I couldn't finish after a one-two with Paul Gascoigne in the Cameroon box.

"People saw me warming up. I was young, they'd heard about me a little bit. And then the crowd started chanting my name. At Wembley! I couldn't believe it."

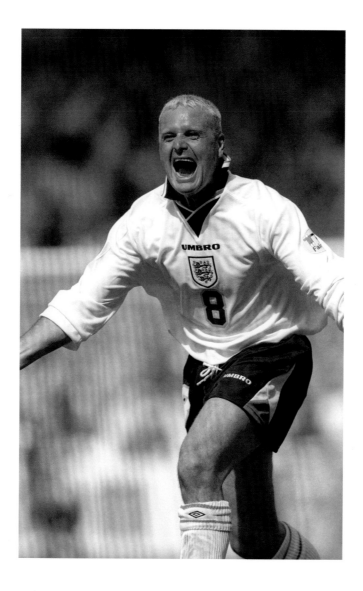

Gazza (above, right) was the one English player you could pick out from the last 20 or 30 years and say he had all the skill to just ghost past players. Incredible strength to go with it. He was an old-fashioned street footballer. When I was an England Youth player, I was invited to train and stay with the England squad during Euro '96. I was meeting my heroes, talking to them, eating with them, training with them: Gazza, Tony Adams, Paul Ince. I played lots of table tennis with Gazza: he used to hold the bat in both hands, like people do in real tennis. In the evenings at the hotel, I'd be phoning up the family and my mates: "You'll never guess who I sat next to at dinner tonight!"

Pace was a big part of my game when I was young. Just as well with Michael Owen about. He was clever, too, so positioning and timing your challenge were just as important. We had some proper characters in the West Ham dressing room back then: Ian Wright and Paolo Di Canio came in, John Moncur, Ian Pearce and 'Razor' Ruddock were already there. And it worked: we ended up fifth in 1998/1999, the club's highest ever Premier League finish.

"All the people I worked with at West Ham were brilliant. They instilled a good work ethic and good football habits in all of us young players, things we've taken with us through our careers."

Racing another quick one: Julian Joachim of Aston Villa (below).
That game was right at the start of 1999/2000, which turned out
to be a memorable season. I played nearly fifty games. We had a
great run in the Intertoto Cup and beat the French side Metz in
the final. Winning it got us into that season's UEFA Cup proper.

Celebrating pogo style (right)! After a good start to the 1999/2000
season, we were struggling: losing games and giving away goals
we shouldn't have been. We weren't happy about it as a team and
I wasn't happy with my own game, either. I knew I still had loads of
work to do developing as a player.

By 2000, the club was standing still a bit. Harry wasn't getting enough funds for transfers and I was put up for sale. In November, I was gone, unveiled as Leeds United's new record signing. I have such good memories of growing up at West Ham: the people, the fans, the atmosphere around the club.

"Every time I think about West Ham it brings a smile to my face and warm feelings. Great times. I owe them a lot."

I eventually cost Leeds £18 million but things didn't start too well. David O'Leary played three at the back to fit me in, we got beaten 3–1 by Leicester in my first game and then, even though I won my fair share of tackles against him (right), James Beattie got the winner for Southampton in my second. But we won one – at last! – at home to Sunderland a week later.

"Leeds chairman Peter Ridsdale put in their bid for me just a week after we'd beaten them 1–0 at Elland Road."

After that dodgy start to my Leeds career, things picked up in the New Year. We played some great football and went 13 games unbeaten in the league. The FA Cup wasn't so great, though. I was used to early exits at West Ham but, after we beat Barnsley in the third round, we fancied ourselves at home to Liverpool. We could have had a couple of penalties early on but, instead, Nick Barmby and Emile Heskey grabbed late goals and we were out.

Giving some back to our travelling fans after a 4–0 win away to Manchester City. I joined some great players at Leeds: Harry Kewell, Alan Smith, my mate Michael Duberry. There were other lads, too, like Jonathan Woodgate, who I also knew from England squads. The Leeds staff, the players and the fantastic supporters at Elland Road made me feel welcome right from the start. I had a brilliant time at the club.

The thing about Leeds was that so many of us were around the same age, our early twenties. That meant when we went out it'd be a dozen of us having a really good time together. When I arrived at Elland Road, Lucas Radebe was the club captain. This selfless man, who'd come from a pretty difficult background, was always smiling, always helping other people. About six months later, when Lucas was getting a few injuries, David O'Leary made me captain. He got the two of us in and explained what he was doing. I wasn't sure at all but Lucas just said: "Take it on from here, Rio." He was really positive about it. Mind you, there was a captain's parking space at the training ground and, even though Lucas said I should use it, I didn't park in it for a good while after! Just didn't feel right somehow.

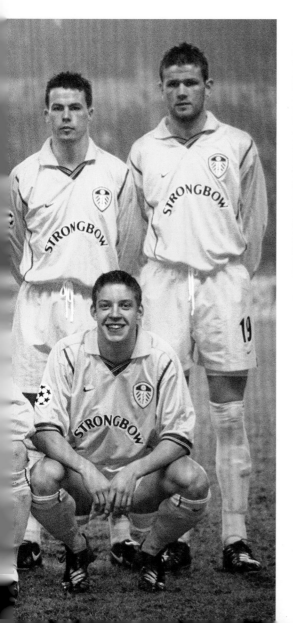

At home in a Champions League quarter-final wasn't a bad time for my first goal in a Leeds shirt. We were already 2–0 up against the Spanish champions, Deportivo de La Coruña. With a quarter of an hour to go, Harry Kewell took a corner and I got myself into some space at the back post. The defender and the keeper got in a mess in front of me and the ball looped up for me to head in. I was loving the chance to play top-level European football. As you can see (above), scoring just made it all feel even better.

"What was I thinking with that celebration? I still don't really know! How are you supposed to react when you score for your country at a World Cup?"

I still pinch myself now: my first England goal was at the World Cup in 2002. Against Denmark in the Round of 16, David Beckham's corner came arcing over towards me and then suddenly, although it wasn't my best ever header, the ball was hitting their keeper and bouncing across the line. That was it: I was off for a disco by the corner flag. Did a Bogle dance, I think. Amazing!

2002/2003

TURNING RED

History echoes around Old Trafford, history written by football's greatest names: Busby, Best, Charlton and Law. United have a tradition of success like no other, the place rings with it. Personally, I knew exactly how good this team I was joining could be: at West Ham I'd been on the wrong end of a 7–1 hiding after we'd made the mistake of scoring first. The chance to move to United was one I knew I had to take.

Games	(Subs)	Goals	Yellow	Red
46	(1)	0	5	0

Final league position: 1st

Champions League finish: Quarter-finalist

Main honours: Premier League title winner.

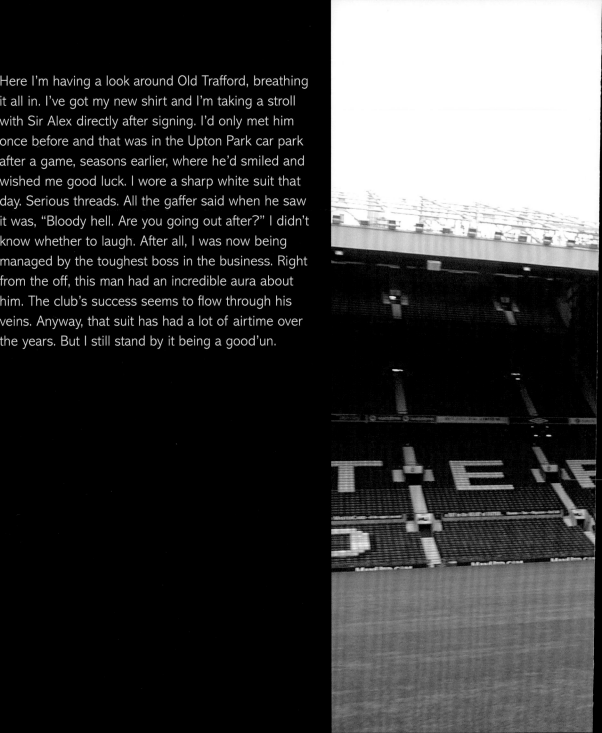

Here I'm having a look around Old Trafford, breathing it all in. I've got my new shirt and I'm taking a stroll with Sir Alex directly after signing. I'd only met him once before and that was in the Upton Park car park after a game, seasons earlier, where he'd smiled and wished me good luck. I wore a sharp white suit that day. Serious threads. All the gaffer said when he saw it was, "Bloody hell. Are you going out after?" I didn't know whether to laugh. After all, I was now being managed by the toughest boss in the business. Right from the off, this man had an incredible aura about him. The club's success seems to flow through his veins. Anyway, that suit has had a lot of airtime over the years. But I still stand by it being a good'un.

At the opening of United's new Academy at Carrington with (from right to left) David May, Sir Bobby Charlton, Sir Alex Ferguson, Nicky Butt and the skipper, Roy Keane. On my very first day training with United, I got it both barrels from Roy. I played a sideways pass when a forward pass was on and he wasn't best pleased. It was like playing with the manager on the pitch with you: Roy always pushed you to be at your bravest and best for the club.

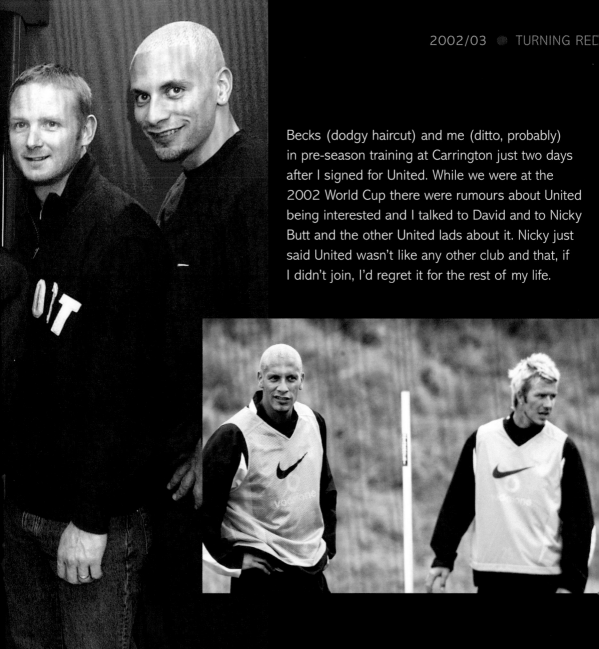

Becks (dodgy haircut) and me (ditto, probably) in pre-season training at Carrington just two days after I signed for United. While we were at the 2002 World Cup there were rumours about United being interested and I talked to David and to Nicky Butt and the other United lads about it. Nicky just said United wasn't like any other club and that, if I didn't join, I'd regret it for the rest of my life.

"The mentality in training at United was totally new to me. The will to win, the desire and the work ethic had to be there every single day. Otherwise you'd be out the door."

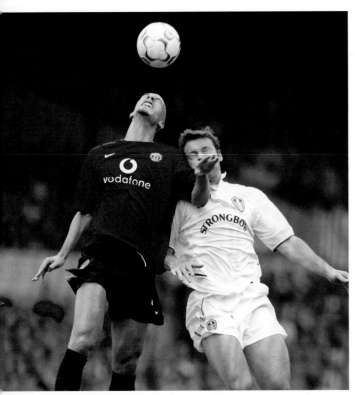

A month into the new season I was back at Elland Road and expecting the worst from the Leeds crowd. There were a few chants – and plenty of boos every time I touched the ball – but it wasn't the nightmare for me that the media hype had claimed it would be. Mind you, Leeds enjoyed themselves. Mark Viduka (above) and company beat us 1-0 and we were left struggling, tenth in the table.

I had aggravation with injuries early on in 02/03: I picked up an ankle knock against Boca Juniors pre-season and missed our opening league games. Then a knee problem kept me out for three games until I came back against Villa in late October. Everything seemed to be working all right, though, when I got the better of Jlloyd Samuel (above) at full stretch!

In terms of results, the start of my first season at United wasn't the best, but after two defeats over Christmas, everything just clicked in 2003. We went unbeaten for the rest of the season and sometimes I just felt like standing and applauding the skill and desire of the players around me: an inch-perfect Beckham cross, a bit of Giggs magic, a perfectly timed van Nistelrooy finish. We reeled in the leaders, Newcastle, and then went up to St James' Park in April and caned them 6–2. It was a big moment: that afternoon we went to the top of the table for the first time all season.

The first time I wore the Number 5 shirt was with England at the 2002 World Cup. That tournament went pretty well for me. It was the first time I really felt comfortable as an England international. After it, I started believing in myself as a player who could compete with the best around. And, because of that experience, the 5 became 'my number'. When I signed at United, I asked the manager who had that shirt. It turned out it was Laurent Blanc (right), and I knew I wasn't going to get it off him. But he was probably about the age I am now, so that was ok: I knew I wouldn't have to wait too long!

We knocked out Leicester, Burnley and Chelsea without conceding a goal in the League Cup. Beating Blackburn over two legs in the semi meant a lot to me: in my first season at United I was into the first domestic cup final of my career (above left).
It turned out to be a disappointing afternoon, though. The atmosphere at the Millennium Stadium was fantastic but we weren't. Still wearing Number 6, I just didn't play well. Not many of us did. And Liverpool beat us 2–0.

"Coming second felt like coming nowhere. I gave my loser's medal to my sister, Sian."

We're lined up for a Champions League game in Germany against Bayer Leverkusen. After the formalities, we won 2–1. Finishing 3rd in the league the season before meant we had to qualify for the group stages and I made my European debut for United in a 5–0 win against Zalaegerszeg of Hungary. We played really well through both of our groups and only lost two out of twelve games. In the quarters, though, we were drawn against the Galácticos: Zidane, Figo, Raúl, Ronaldo and Roberto Carlos. Real Madrid were a half-decent side!

"I knew United were capable of winning the league and the Champions League. It's what I'd joined to be a part of."

As a kid growing up in Peckham, watching World Cups on TV, all I did was dream about playing against Brazil. I got my wish when I took on Ronaldo in Japan in 2002. Ten months later, he was lined up against me again, this time in the white of Real Madrid. Real made us suffer at the Bernabéu and beat us 3–1 in the first leg, but we hadn't given up on clawing them back. As it turned out, it was an unbelievable game at Old Trafford and we scored four on the night. A hat-trick from Ronaldo, though, meant Real won 6–5 on aggregate. He got a standing ovation from the United crowd when he was subbed. Classy touch from our fans, but they were as gutted as we were not to have gone through.

"If it hadn't been for his knee injuries, I think Ronaldo might have gone down as the best player ever. After he lost that yard of pace, maybe we all lost sight of just how good he'd been."

I look at a photo like this and think what a privilege it's been to work and play alongside these lads for so long. We're celebrating a Ruud van Nistelrooy hat-trick at Fulham in March. Flying. After we beat Charlton on May 3 in our last-but-one game, we were eight points clear of Arsenal who had to win at Leeds the following day to stay in with a chance. I couldn't face watching the game on TV and just paced around the house waiting for the result. I'd never sweated like that over a game but my old team-mates didn't let me down. They beat Arsenal 3–2. United were champions and, for the first time in my career, I was a champion too.

"When you get your hands on that trophy, you do the things any kid would do: lift it up, feel the weight of it, polish up the shine, show it off to the fans!"

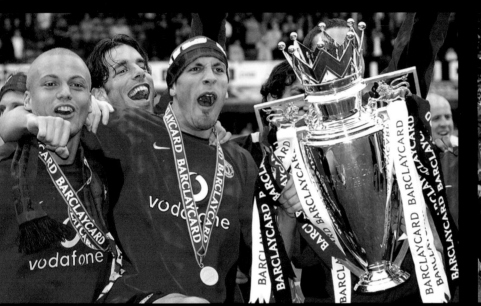

Sunday May 11, 2003. Last game of the season, away to Everton. I'll never forget it. And I'll never know how we managed to win 2–1 on the day, either: we'd done plenty of celebrating during the week! It might have been better to have lifted up the trophy in front of 60,000 Reds at Old Trafford but I wasn't complaining. After seven years as a pro, this was it: what every player wants. And I was drinking in every last moment in the Merseyside sunshine.

2003/2004

ON THE SIDELINES

I couldn't wait for this new season. The excitement of how the last one had finished was still pulsing in my veins. We did a pre-season tour in the US — something completely new for me — and I was in really good nick. I was all set for another season to remember, but this one didn't go United's way. Or Rio Ferdinand's either. Even playing for one of the world's greatest clubs, you have your downs as well as ups.

Games	(Subs)	Goals	Yellow	Red
27	(0)	0	1	0

Final league position: 3rd

Champions League finish: Round of 16

Main honours: Community Shield winner, FA Cup winner

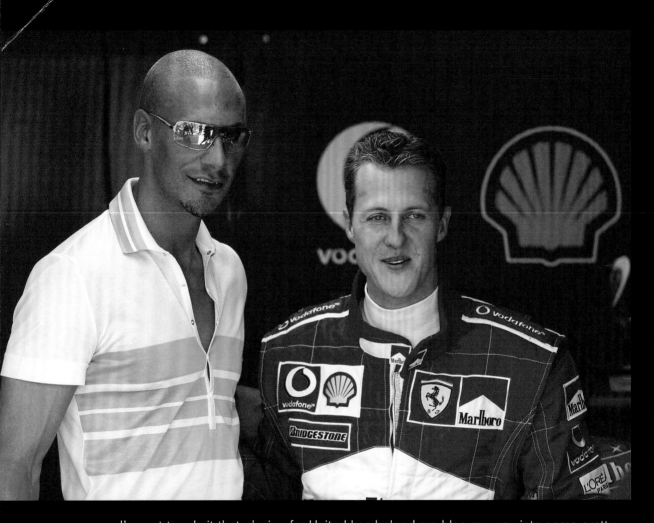

I've got to admit that playing for United has helped me blag my way into some pretty amazing places. In the summer of 2003, not only did I get the chance to watch the Monaco Grand Prix but I also spent time in the pit lane with Michael Schumacher (above) and the Ferrari team. I've always liked a nice motor, ever since I bought my first – a Ford Fiesta, as you're asking – when I was still a teenager at West Ham. That Monaco trip got even better when I was lent a luxury yacht and took a few old mates from Peckham out on the Med for ten days. Like the lottery bloke says: Welcome to my world!

Training in America was great but, blimey, it was hot (left). In the middle of the summer we went on a big US tour. It couldn't have gone much better: we beat Celtic by four in Seattle, Club America of Mexico 3–1 in LA, then Juventus 4–1 in New Jersey and, finally, Barcelona 3–1 in Philadelphia. By the time we headed home for the Community Shield, we were buzzing.

"Thousands of Man United fans turn out when we play overseas: it feels like the club and the players are giving them something back for their support over the years."

The first team squad for the 2003/2004 season (below). That summer, we'd lost Becks to Real Madrid and Juan Verón to Chelsea, but the club had brought five new players in, including a Portuguese fella named Cristiano Ronaldo. We had played his club Sporting Lisbon in a friendly and we could all see that this tall, skinny kid was amazing. I wasn't the only one saying we should sign him! A week later he was a United player, although he was signed too late for the squad photo and too late to play in the Community Shield. That was my second United trophy (right) and – sort of! – my first United goal: in the penalty shootout against Arsenal, I took and scored our second.

We couldn't wait for the season to get started and, when it did, we came out punching and won our first three games. The new boys were settling in and we played some really good football. In fact, we only lost one in our first nine. August 2003 was a big month for the whole Ferdinand family: my little brother, Anton, made his West Ham debut against Preston in the Championship. Go on, bro'!

"It was always going to be hard work to get the chance to play at a club like United. Once you're there, it's even harder: you have to stay there and meet the manager's and the supporters' expectations."

I started out playing in midfield as a kid. I always felt comfortable on the ball. And I still like to help dictate the game when I can, carrying the ball out from the back (like against Spurs, above) or finding a long pass (as I am against Newcastle, right). When we won at Spurs in November 2003, it took us top of the table for the first time that season, a point clear of Arsenal.

There are games that have meant a lot to me for personal reasons, like when I went back to Elland Road for the second time and we won. No wonder I'm all over Roy Keane (left) after he scored the winner. Then there are other games that mean more than most for the club and the supporters. They don't get bigger – or more intense – than Liverpool v United. The rivalry goes back such a long way and, when we go to Anfield, we know what to expect from their team and their fans. We're always desperate for a result and so are the travelling Reds. Look at the pure delight (above) after Giggsy scored one of his two goals that won us the game in November 2003. Can't beat it!

The club skipper presents me with a framed shirt (right) signed by football legends including Bryan Robson and Sir Bobby Charlton… Oh yeah, and also by Roy himself! I'd bid the highest for it during a charity auction at the United for UNICEF dinner in September. Man U has raised more than £2.5 million for the charity, which does amazing work to improve the lives of the world's most deprived children. The shirt joined my nice little collection at home, including shirts from Paul Gascoigne, Roberto Baggio, Luís Figo, and a Michael Jordan basketball vest, as well as my very first team shirt from Bloomfield Athletic.

"I'm proud of the fact that the club, the players and the staff give so much support to charities and projects both at home and abroad."

In the Champions League, we were doing all right. We beat Panathanaikos 5–0 and then won twice against Rangers in what the papers were calling 'The Battle of Britain'. We topped the group and drew José Mourinho's Porto in the first knockout round. I was sat in the stands: we were leading on away goals until the 90th minute when Francisco Costinha scored. A sickener. I'm an even worse loser when I'm watching than I am out on the pitch. I just shut down after a defeat. Don't even think about talking to me until the following day.

That game was infamous for Mourinho's big knee-slide celebration down the touchline in his suit. I don't really know José Mourinho, but I've met him a few times. I was in Madrid last season to watch Cristiano play at the Bernabéu and I saw Mourinho beforehand. He's always struck me as a polite, open type of guy. And I'll tell you: he's got a sense of humour. You know, he's been very successful and you have to respect how he's won things everywhere he's managed. But he likes a laugh; likes taking the mickey!

I was out of football for eight months from January 2004. It could have finished me if I'd sat at home thinking about it. But the manager and the lads were superb for me. Supported me all the way: United by name, United by nature. We stand by our own especially when it gets difficult. I just trained my way through it. I don't think I've ever worked so hard, like here (above, right) with first team coach Mike Phelan, Gary and Phil Neville, Scholesy and John O'Shea.

"One of the great strengths of our club is that there are no cliques at United. It's one of the squad's best qualities: on the pitch and off, we're all in it together."

I went to each and every remaining game of the season at Old Trafford, and most of the away games as well. It was odd being suited-up when the team were out on the pitch, frustrating that I couldn't get out there and help out. We finished third in the league behind Arsenal (champions) and Chelsea, and that hurt. But I did enjoy our FA Cup semi-final win over Arsenal (above), even if I couldn't play in the final itself where the lads cruised past Millwall, 3–0. I watched so many FA Cup Finals as a kid, it stung that I couldn't get out there and join in. I still feel like there's a bit of a hole in my career that only an FA Cup winner's medal can fill.

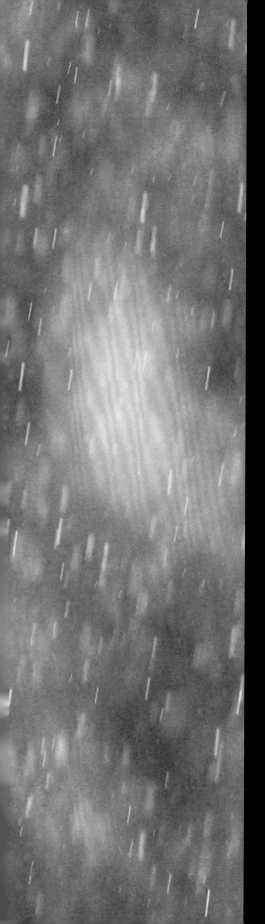

2004/2005

BACK IN THE GAME

Eight months out felt like a lifetime. I literally counted down the days, getting more excited and more impatient the nearer I got to being able to play for United again. I felt fit, even though I hadn't had games, but I was nervous as well to be honest. What would it be like stepping back in at the top level with the season already underway? I was lucky: I had my own strength of mind and I had my team-mates and the boss. I was always intent on rising to the challenge.

Games	(Subs)	Goals	Yellow	Red
43	(0)	0	3	0

Final league position: 3rd
Champions League finish: Round of 16
Main honours: PFA Team of the Year

Seat too small or bloke too big (above)? A club like United puts the miles in and we were back in the US in the summer of 2004. The games weren't great: we lost on pens to Bayern Munich and AC Milan. But everything else on that trip was good: we did loads of media, put on coaching clinics and met hundreds of unbelievably enthusiastic kids, some of whom could play a bit too. Just look at that picture (left): don't try and tell me that Americans aren't loving the beautiful game.

The gaffer had said that as soon as I was available, he'd put me into a game. So I knew I had to be right mentally as well as physically. I worked with a sports psychologist, Keith Power, and one of the things we used was visualisation. I still use those techniques now when preparing for games. It's always been important for me to start games well. If I do that, I usually go on to play well the whole game. So, the night before, before I go to sleep, I'll try and visualise my first touch of the ball, my first tackle. I'll try to imagine a ball being played down a channel behind me and me recovering and winning it back. I'll go through that process again first thing in the morning and then, again, in the dressing room just before kick-off.

"I just want to win. All the time. Even if I lose a game in training, it ruins my day. Like I say: losing's something I've never been good at."

Wayne Rooney arrived at Old Trafford that summer (above). And got plenty of stick in training after signing for United in a disastrous blue-and-grey striped jumper. Not that Wazza was bothered. He just fitted straight in even though he was young and there were some pretty big personalities in the dressing room. Me, I just grafted: training as hard as I could to be as fit as I could without actually playing in games.

What a game to come back in: Liverpool at home. I got out on the pitch and all my nerves disappeared. One early tackle and suddenly the whole of Old Trafford was chanting my name. The crowd were great: carried me through the 90, really. I got Man of the Match even though, any other day, that would have been Mikael Silvestre, who got the goals that won us the match. Then five days later I was at White Hart Lane and Jermain Defoe gave me a proper game. (No wonder: I heard after that the England manager, Sven-Göran Eriksson, had been in the crowd.) What mattered was the clean sheet in a 1–0 win thanks to Ruud van Nistelrooy's penalty just on half-time. Back in the thick of it, I just loved being able to play football again.

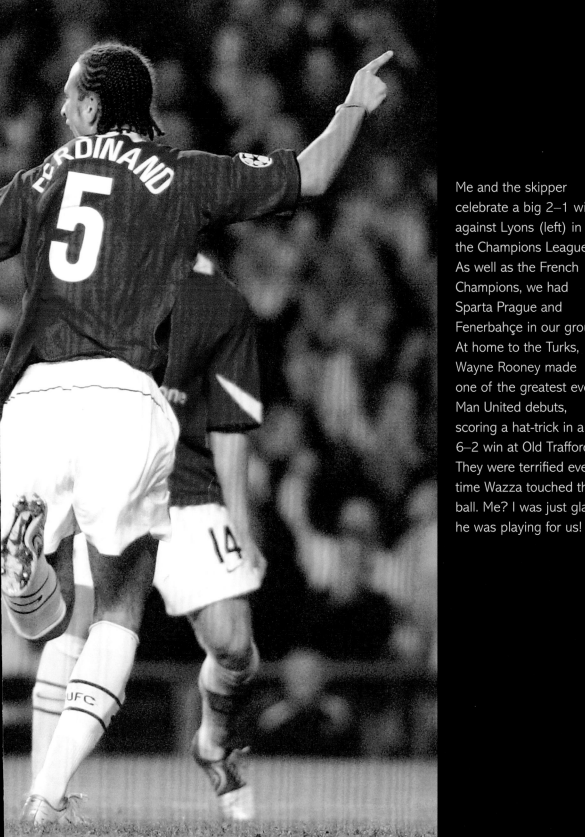

Me and the skipper celebrate a big 2–1 win against Lyons (left) in the Champions League. As well as the French Champions, we had Sparta Prague and Fenerbahçe in our group. At home to the Turks, Wayne Rooney made one of the greatest ever Man United debuts, scoring a hat-trick in a 6–2 win at Old Trafford. They were terrified every time Wazza touched the ball. Me? I was just glad he was playing for us!

Arsenal at Old Trafford is always a big game. Rivalry between the players matched by rivalry between the managers: Arsène Wenger and Sir Alex. They arrived that October top of the league, unbeaten in the whole of the previous season, dubbing themselves 'The Invincibles' and looking to stretch their incredible run to 50 games. The gaffer wasn't having it. He picked a really attacking team. And we really attacked: Ruud scored a penalty and then Wayne, on his 19th birthday, got the second which killed off the game and the Gunners.

Emile Heskey (above): a massively underrated player. Real hard, physical work for a centre half and just great for a strike partner: he'd take all the knocks and make room – at club or international level – for someone else to go and get the goals and the glory. Mind you, I did him here at St Andrews against Birmingham City, and he didn't score either. Trouble was, neither did we. It was one of five draws in seven games, a run that did us no favours in the title race that autumn.

Scan this page to hear Giggs speak about Rio

I love football: doing my job as a defender, but coming out and playing a bit too. Especially in front of a packed Old Trafford: against Southampton (above), a little burst gets me away from Kevin Phillips and Dexter Blackstock; and (right) I get the ball down with the outside of my foot during a victory over Bolton. By the New Year I was flying, couldn't wait for the next game. We got a bit of a shock in the FA Cup – Conference side Exeter held us to a draw at Old Trafford in the third round – but pushed on from that and, four months later, I was walking out for the final at Cardiff. The afternoon was a massive disappointment though: we completely outplayed Arsenal for 120 minutes – I even had a goal disallowed – but lost on penalties.

"The whole season we defended really well as a team. Gave up just 26 goals in 38 league games. That's a brick wall, by the way!"

We lost 1–0 at home to AC Milan in the Champions League in February. They were the best European team I'd ever played against but we were Manchester United. I thought we could do something at the San Siro, knew we'd create chances. Credit to them though, all their big players showed up for it: Kaká, Hernán Crespo (above), Clarence Seedorf and Paolo Maldini. Maldini was marking Cristiano Ronaldo – a 36-year-old trying to keep up with a 20-year-old – and he was brilliant. Experience makes a difference: I understand that myself now! Milan beat us 1–0 again and me, Scholesy and the boys had to take it on the chin. Another Champions League campaign had ended too early.

We went 20 games unbeaten in the league either side of Christmas. And 14 of those games were clean sheets by the way! We did Arsenal at Highbury and were feeling invincible by the time we got to Craven Cottage in the middle of March. Cristiano got the winner that afternoon (below) but it was the end of the run. We drew at home to Blackburn then lost a couple, away to Norwich and Everton. Suddenly it wasn't looking too clever for us at the top of the table.

Ronny used to beat his man and then come back and beat him again, just for fun. And everything he did he did at pace, which made him impossible to play against at times."

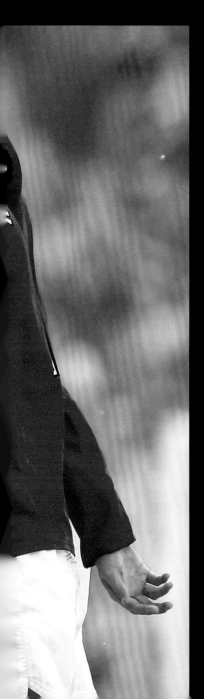

When Ronaldo first started training with us, we could all see he had phenomenal talent. The real thing with Ronny was his work ethic, his complete dedication. People have this idea of what he's like from watching him play but I can tell you he's a completely different animal off the pitch compared to on it. When he's playing, he's got that desire and competitiveness that maybe make him seem arrogant, make it look as if he's snarling through games sometimes. But if you know Ronny, you know he's just a very funny, normal lad; well, normal except for the looks and the money! When he was at United he always wanted to be in on the practical jokes and the mickey-taking. And he was always the first one ready to laugh at himself.

"I made the PFA Team of the Year at the end of the season. It didn't make up for only finishing third in the league."

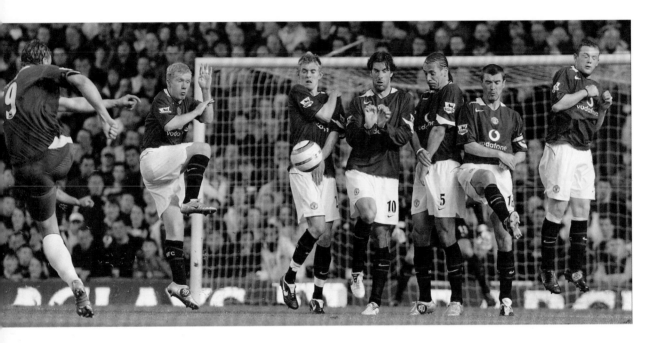

Chelsea beat us first game of the season and knocked us out of the League Cup after José Mourinho had accused us of getting at the ref. So, when we went to Stamford Bridge in May – even though the title had gone – we were after a bit of revenge as well as the win. Ruud scored early on and you can see what that meant to us (right). But Chelsea ended up winning and those three points helped them beat our record Premier League total of 92. Every knock-back is a challenge for us at United, though.

2005/2006

SEASON OF FIRSTS

Times were changing at Old Trafford. We signed two new keepers – Edwin van der Sar and Ben Foster – and a true United legend, Roy Keane, left the club. For better and worse, it turned out to be a season of firsts for me: a first domestic cup win, my first league goals for United and even a first chance to line up opposite my little brother, Anton. It was also the season, though, when I was red-carded for the first – and only – time in my professional career.

Games	(Subs)	Goals	Yellow	Red
52	(2)	3	2	1

Final league position: 2nd

Champions League finish: Group stage

Main honours: League Cup winner

I scored my first Premier League goal for United in December 2005 against Wigan, a header from a Ryan Giggs corner. I lost it completely, celebrating; well you would, wouldn't you, in front of a packed Old Trafford and after not scoring for 140 games? After that, there was no stopping me: a fortnight later I got another (left, both pictures) against West Brom. Another Giggsy corner: up I go and, this time, a perfect connection.

"Scoring goals, in front of 70,000 people? It's what kids dream about. It's what me and my mates used to dream about, kicking a ball around on the Friary Estate. I've been lucky and had those dreams come true."

Nobody told me and Wayne it was black-tie! Even so, we had a great time (both pictures) with the kids at Victoria Park Junior School in Stretford, just round the corner from the ground. It was part of a Sport For All scheme aimed at getting children into sport and out of trouble. United do a lot of work in the local community and I've always been up for some of that. I used to volunteer for community work when I was a teenager at West Ham. Football clubs owe a lot to the communities they're part of.

"It's about remembering where you're from and, hopefully, inspiring kids like the kid you were to go and make something of themselves."

Crouchy (left) is tall, isn't he? And I'm standing on tiptoe! There's always that passion and edge to United v Liverpool, so my third goal for the club was very special indeed. A header in the 90th minute to beat them at Old Trafford? In front of the Stretford End, with our lot going bananas? You cannot possibly put into words how that feels. Absolutely phenomenal. And then I went and did it again the following season, didn't I? Touch on the right foot, half-volley with the left. Top corner. Beautiful. Every game against them is special. So is beating them.

"Scoring against Liverpool (above) is about
as good as being a footballer gets."

In January 2006, we played Blackburn Rovers in the
semi-finals of the Carling Cup. There was a bit of
tension between me and Robbie Savage: I told him
to stop acting up to get free kicks, and he took
offence. We played Blackburn again in the league
a week later. I was playing in midfield, running the
game, when Savage thought he'd bring theatre to
the football ground once again. He pretended I'd
kicked him and went down. I couldn't believe it. But
the ref bought it, showed me a second yellow card
and then the dreaded red. It was the first and only
time I've been sent off as a professional footballer.

Well someone's got to get the bottle open, haven't they? Here we're spraying the bubbly about after beating Wigan 4–0 in the Carling Cup Final. It was my first cup with United and the first time the club had won that trophy since 1992. Giggsy played in both games: that seemed like a long career even then and, of course, he's still going strong! The message on our T-shirts was for Alan Smith, who broke his leg a week previously in an FA Cup defeat against Liverpool.

"There's no point getting to a final unless you come away with the cup. Second place doesn't get you into the United history books, does it?"

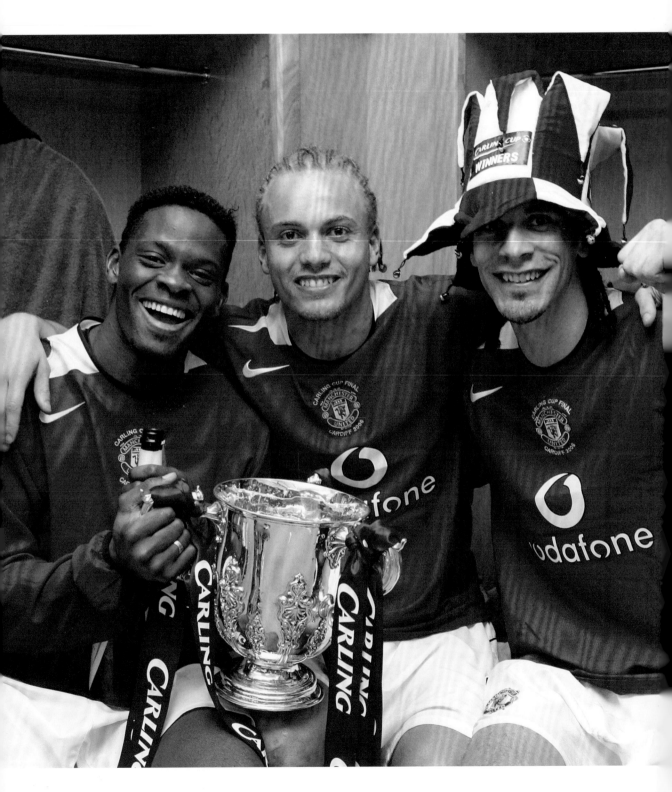

I think I must have been wearing that hat for a bet (left). Mind you, nobody's thinking straight after winning a final. Down in the dressing room at the Millennium Stadium, me, Wes Brown and Louis Saha made sure we got our hands on the cup. Louis scored against Wigan as well as in four of the five rounds getting to Cardiff. He was probably the hardest person I've ever played against in training. Defenders just bounced off him and he didn't even notice if you kicked him. Pace, two good feet, great runs off the ball and a shot like a cannon: Louis had the lot.

Super skills on display at the Carrington training ground (left). Great fun. We often welcome visitors or go to see schools in the local area. I'm playing keepy-uppy here with some young kids from Manchester to help improve their cushioning and ball control skills. Some days I think I want to be a coach in the future and work with young kids and youth teams. Other days, I think I would prefer to become a senior-team manager. Anyway, no need to make that decision just yet.

"If I hadn't been a professional footballer, I would have worked in youth clubs or for the local council, with kids. That's what a lot of my old friends do."

Old Trafford's a fantastic arena even when there's nobody there. When you walk out of the tunnel before a game, though, the place seems to grow. I remember going there as an away player and being really intimidated, thinking I'd be happy getting out with a draw. It's a hard place to get anything, especially if United score first. Now, as a United player, I draw on all that: the confidence, the history, having that fantastic crowd on your side.

Scan this page to hear Anton speak about Rio

When we were kids, there was a bit of open space between our block on the estate and the next one. We used to call it 'The Back Grass'. I used to go down there with my little brother, Anton, and we'd play: me versus him and his mate. I never, ever, let them win! But I've always wanted him to be the best player he could be, which is why I'm more nervous if I'm watching him play than I ever am playing myself. All those years later – brotherly love, eh? – and we're arguing the toss when West Ham came to Old Trafford in April 2006 (right). The fixture at Upton Park earlier in the season had been our first against each other as pros and the crowd gave both of us a great reception that day. We won, though. London and Manchester. Some things never change: I couldn't let Anton win, could I?

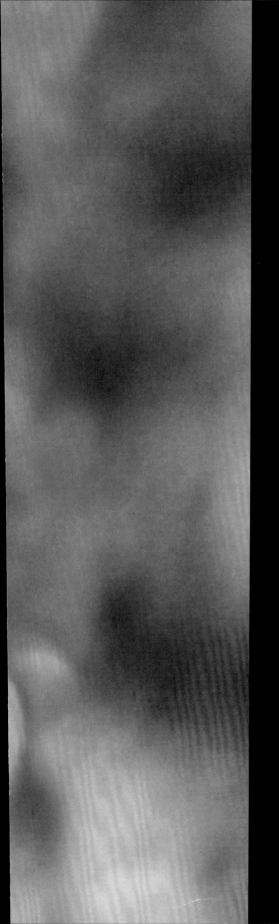

2006/2007

CHASING TITLES

We finished behind Chelsea two seasons in a row after winning the title in my first season at Old Trafford. We all knew it wasn't good enough and it hurt us: the supporters, the boss and the players as well. Our number one priority that season was to win the Premier League. Of course that's what we aim for every season. Looking around the squad during pre-season, I was absolutely convinced that, in 2006/2007, we could do it. And we did.

Games	(Subs)	Goals	Yellow	Red
49	(1)	1	3	0

Final league position: 1st

Champions League finish: Semi-finalist

Main honours: Premier League title winner; PFA Team of the Year.

Trouble comes in all shapes and sizes. You get the tricky ones, like Freddie Ljungberg of Arsenal (above), and you get the ones who are all about power, like Chelsea's Didier Drogba (left), who I voted for as PFA Player of the Year. It wasn't just his 33 goals; he was a battering ram for Chelsea all season long. To win the title, you have to deal with them all and we made a good start, beating Fulham 5–1 on the opening day and then losing just once in the next 17 games.

We won 1–0 at the Estádio da Luz against Benfica in the
Champions League. Nemanja Vidic and I got used to keeping
clean sheets with Edwin van der Sar in goal behind us.
Great shot-stopper, great talker and great temperament. Edwin
was the coolest keeper I've ever played in front of. A great kicker
of the ball too: because he was two-footed, you knew you could
give it back to him and get on with the game; Edwin would always
find a decent pass!

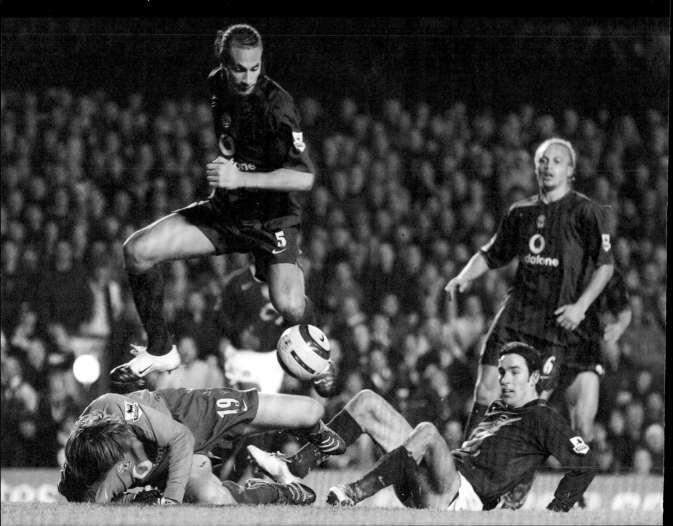

"Giggsy's perfect: athletic, skilful, hard-working, intelligent. And he's been at the top for 20 years plus. One of the very best I've played with."

Ryan's a phenomenon. He's developed his game so he can play anywhere and, apparently, for ever! Never seen anything like him and don't expect to ever again. We had Giggsy for inch-perfect corners and Cristiano Ronaldo to take free kicks. Celtic had Shunsuke Nakamura (above, left). He scored against us home and away in the Champions League that season, and we went into our last group game needing to beat Benfica at Old Trafford to qualify. We won 3–2 after going behind, and a Ryan Giggs goal turned out to be the winner (above, right).

I've just done Anton with a little drop of the shoulder (left) and what does he do? Once I was away, I know him so I knew what was coming. If he hadn't fouled me and stopped me, he'd never have heard the last of it! We're that competitive we'll never speak before a game against each other. It was the same with my cousin, Les. We might say a 'well done' afterwards but beforehand all we're thinking about is winning. I'm a bad loser anyway and West Ham beating us twice that season killed me. If we draw or lose at Upton Park I don't go anywhere near their Players' Lounge. I'm headphones on, straight on to the United bus.

After knocking out Lille, we were drawn against Roma in the Champions League quarter-finals. They won 2–1 at the Stadio Olimpico but we gave them a game and fancied our chances in the second leg. What a night that was. Outstanding. The manager said afterwards: "You'll never get a moment like this again in your careers." We won 7–1: everything we tried seemed to come off. Everybody played well, all the training ground preparation worked and there were 74,000 there to enjoy it. One of the great Old Trafford nights of all time. It played like a dream.

"Whatever we tried on the pitch came off, everyone was an 8 or 9 out of 10. It was almost the perfect football match."

Doors to manual. Prepare for take-off. I'm beating Portsmouth's Matt Taylor to the ball all day long (left). And a couple of goals from Wazza meant we won the game as well. That was in the fourth round. We also saw off Villa, Reading and Middlesbrough before battering Watford 4–1 (above) in the semi. I was desperate to be an FA Cup winner after missing the final against Millwall in 2004. The fixture was back at the new Wembley Stadium too: there was a proper sense of occasion. It was a really tight game until Drogba scored for Chelsea with four minutes of extra-time left. Devastating.

One thing you can count on with a Manchester United team: we'll never give up. It's one of the reasons we score so many late goals. That's part of the deal here from the moment you sign. Last few months of the league season, they all felt like big games. And we wanted to win every single one: that's desire with a big D. We got fours against Spurs, Watford, Bolton and Blackburn but, even in the tight games, we found a way. At Anfield, it was John O'Shea – genius! – getting the last-minute winner. When Ronny did the same against Fulham at Craven Cottage (right), we were all up for a party on the touchline!

"United's will to win stems from the manager. And it filters down through the players and the staff and into every youngster at the Academy."

You can see I was in the mood (left), easing away from Stewart Downing and Andy Taylor. The Old Trafford crowd expected a win against Middlesbrough and so did we, especially after Kieran Richardson gave us the lead (below). But Boro hung in and, near the end of the first half, I tweaked my groin and signalled to the bench for treatment. Moments later, my old team-mate from Leeds, Mark Viduka, got in between me and Wes Brown to score. The frustration was knowing that if I'd been fit I'd have cleared the danger, no problem. Instead, Boro held on and came away with a point.

So nearly, so nearly... I head the ball onto Man City's crossbar after Giggsy's corner had been flicked on by Cristiano Ronaldo – towards the back post (left). The Manchester derby in May wasn't a classic and early on Ronny had been stamped on by a City player, but the ref didn't see it. Ronny got his revenge with a first-half penalty that gave us an unbelievably crucial three points. You can see how exhilarated I was at the end of the game (above). We all knew that Chelsea now had to beat Arsenal the following day to keep the title race alive.

Don't get me wrong, I enjoy training most days. But Monday mornings aren't usually this much fun: on the Sunday, Arsenal held Chelsea 1–1 at the Emirates and that meant the title was ours. Somebody from Barclays, the Premier League sponsors, made the mistake of dropping champagne off for us at Carrington. I gave this bottle a proper shake-up first: it felt fantastic to have the title back where it belonged. Eight of the 11 players in the PFA Team of the Year were from United, including me and the rest of the manager's first-choice back five. Everything came together brilliantly for us that year.

"The way I spray the champagne about, I should have been a Formula One driver. Let's get this party started!"

2007/2008

THE ULTIMATE DOUBLE

Being league champions again felt good. Really good. And the United way has always been to push on from success, to try and have that feeling year in, year out. We wanted to win it again. And we knew the manager wanted us to realise our potential in Europe as well. He brought in new talent: Nani, Anderson, Carlos Tevez. We were ready to go again. And maybe ready to go one better.

Games	(Subs)	Goals	Yellow	Red
51	(0)	3	6	0

Final league position: 1st

Champions League finish: Winner

Main honours: Premier League title winner; UEFA Champions League winner; Community Shield winner; PFA Team of the Year; FIFPro World XI.

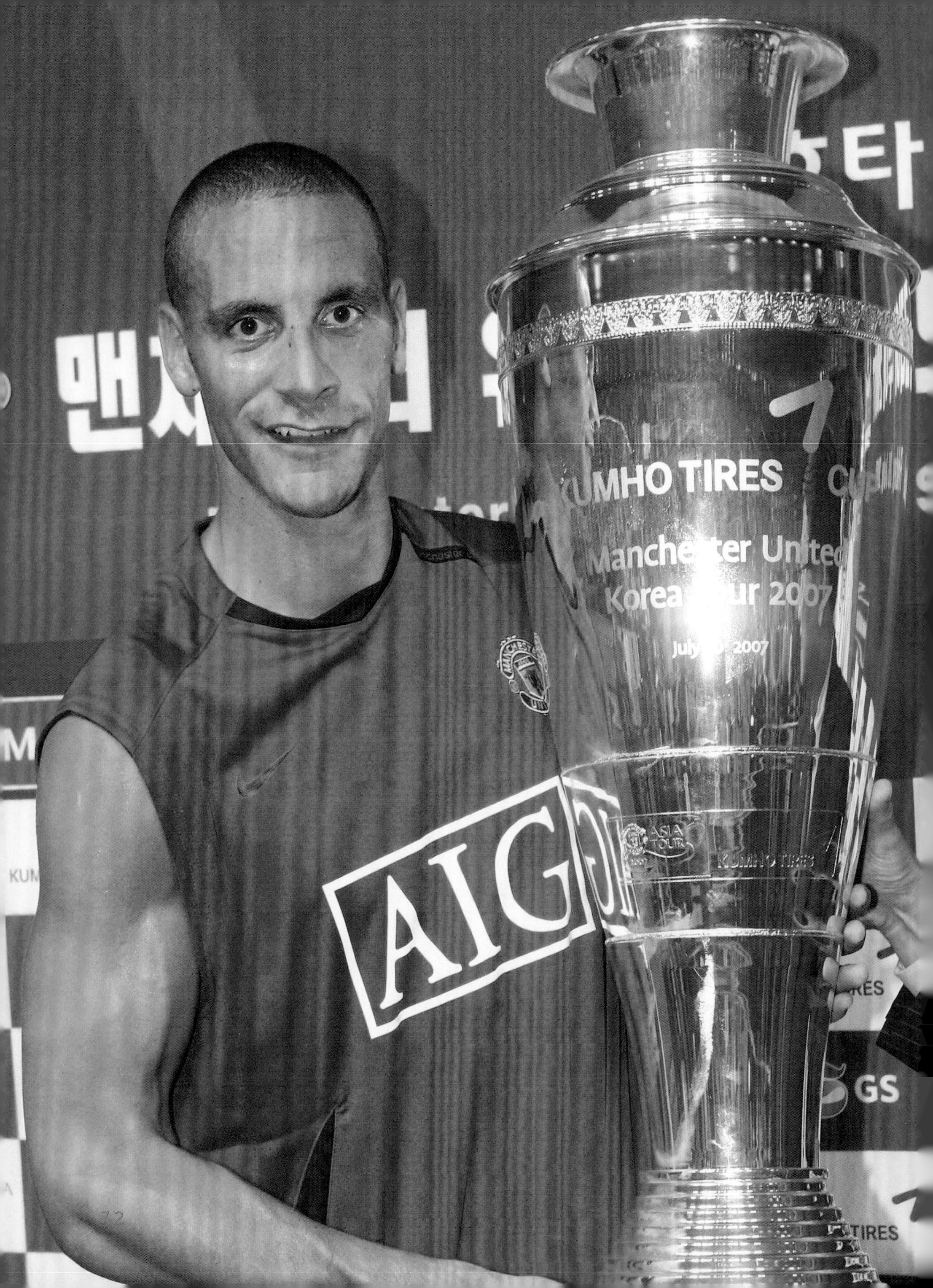
KUMHO TIRES
AIG
GS

Maybe we're unusual, but at United we genuinely enjoy pre-season tours. You find yourself in different cultures, surrounded by different people, even eating different food! Not that there's ever much time for sight-seeing. In 2007 we were in the Far East for four matches in 12 days, including one against FC Seoul of South Korea. Winning that game won us the Kumho Tires Cup (left), which I managed to pose with thanks to a little help from some bloke in a pin-stripe suit. Couple of days later, we'd arrived at Guangzhou Airport (above, left) for a game that saw us lead out some of the tiniest mascots ever – local schoolchildren – at the Guangdong Olympic Stadium (above right).

"I love Asia. I love Asian Reds, too: crazy for United and loyal as they come. We can go out, meet them, sign autographs. We recognise their support and they deserve to see us giving something back."

We played Chelsea in the Community Shield, with the game held at Wembley Stadium for the first time since 2000. Back then, it had also been us against Chelsea. They'd beaten us 2–0 and we weren't in the mood for a repeat. It finished 1–1. I took our first penalty in the shoot-out: bottom left corner, job done. And then it became the Edwin van der Sar show. He saved Chelsea's first three so, by the time Michael Carrick (below) and Wayne Rooney had scored, it was all over. Plenty of time left for celebrating in the dressing room with the silverware, with me making sure I'm next to the top man in the photo!

Scan this page
to hear Carrick
speak about Rio

"I played 51 games in 2007/2008,
more than any other United player."

I felt I was right on my game, first kick till last. We had a shocking start
and were 17th in the table after two draws and a defeat in our first three
league games. Eight straight wins soon put that right, though, including
a 1–0 at Goodison Park (below) thanks to a Nemanja Vidic goal. I was
on the scoresheet a month later, in a 4–1 win at Villa Park. Me and
the big fella don't just defend, you know...

Attacking again (right), this time against big
Chris Samba. Blackburn were on a roll and
had won seven in eight before they came to
Old Trafford in November. But two goals in as
many minutes from Ronny settled it and made
it ten games unbeaten for us. The run ended
the following week, though, when we lost 1–0
at Bolton. The goal scorer at the Reebok was
Nicolas Anelka, who would turn up playing for
another team against us later in the season.

Two days before facing Arsenal away and I'm meeting children from St. Andrew's School in Boothstown, west of Salford and a heartland of Reds fans. I even get time for a bit of coaching with some of the kids. Witness the drama (right) as a young lad misses a free header! He'll go far. It was all part of the work the Manchester United Foundation does locally in Greater Manchester schools, youth groups and out-of-school centres, particularly with kids from deprived areas. I'm very happy to be a part of it.

"I try to tell kids, if you have a focus and a real intention to make something of yourself, it's always possible."

The team, the manager and the whole ground observe a minute's silence on 10th February 2008. It was the Old Trafford game closest to the 50th anniversary of the Munich Air Disaster in which 23 people died, including many of the talented young United team the world knows as the Busby Babes. The game that followed was the Manchester derby.

"There were fears that City fans might disrupt the moment, but they were top drawer on the day. There was total respect."

No, your eyes aren't deceiving you. That's me in goal in our FA Cup sixth round game versus Portsmouth. It had nearly happened at White Hart Lane the season before – I'd even had the jersey and gloves on in that game, before the gaffer gave John O'Shea the nod instead. I was the third United goalkeeper of the game against Portsmouth, after Edwin had gone off injured and our substitute keeper, Tomasz Kuszczak, got red-carded. I went in goal for the resulting penalty. I made a shocking dive and failed to save Sulley Muntari's effort. I think I managed one actual save later on but we lost 1–0 and were out of the cup. Being in goal is a lonely place, I can tell you.

"Ronny didn't just arrive out of nowhere. He wasn't just born one of the world's best players. Everything he's achieved, everything he's won, has been down to him working and training incredibly hard to develop an unbelievable talent."

We went into 2008 neck and neck with Chelsea at the top of the table. Cristiano Ronaldo was having an unbelievable season. Seemed like he was scoring every week. He got a hat-trick at home to Newcastle and then got one at Reading, after I'd done all the hard work (left). One of the best of the lot was a towering header in a 3–0 win over Liverpool at Old Trafford. Oh, we celebrated that one (above)! Thirty-one league goals won Ronny the Golden Boot, but the team's defending – just 22 conceded – was just as important as we hunted down the title.

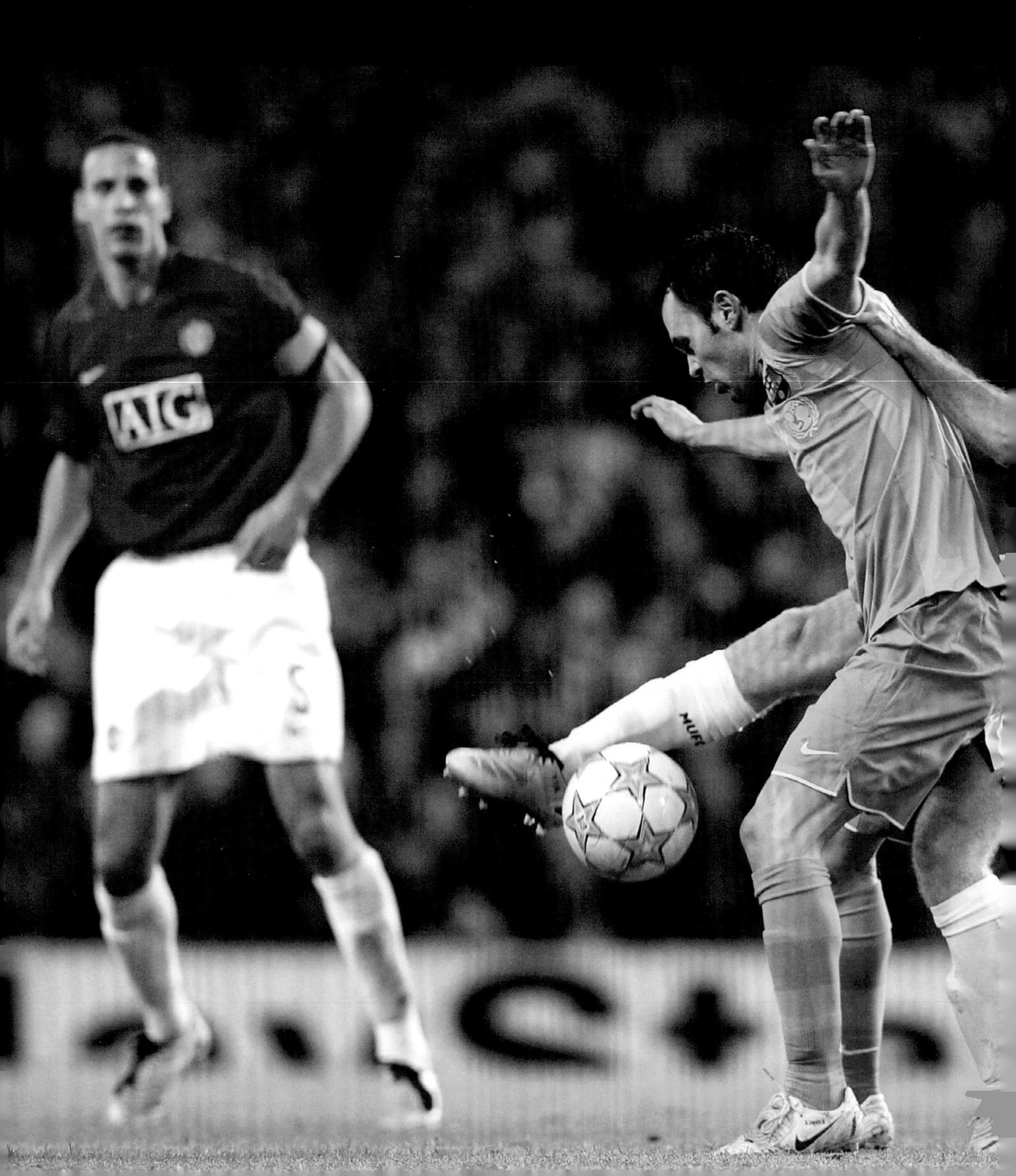
AIG

We knocked out Lyon and Roma on our way to
the Champions League semi against a Barcelona
team full of world class talents like Andrés Iniesta
(left), Xavi Hernández and Lionel Messi. It was
Scholesy, though, who got the only goal of the
two legs, a 25-yard bullet at Old Trafford.

Then domestic rivals became European rivals: it was Chelsea in
the final. Leading the team out as captain at the Luzhniki Stadium
in Moscow was perhaps my proudest ever moment in football. An
unbelievable night for me personally, as well as for the club. We
should have had the game won by half-time in Moscow. We missed
chances and Cech kept Chelsea in it. And then they got stronger in
the second half until we were hanging on a bit by the end (above).

Shoot-outs are always nail-biting but what was at stake here made it almost unbearable.

After nine of the ten mandatory penalties, the scores were 4–4 but Chelsea still had their last kick to take. If their skipper John Terry scored, the cup was theirs. Unfortunately for him, his foot slipped just as he struck the ball and he hit the post. We had been gifted a second chance.

At 6–5 to us, Nicolas Anelka – him again! – went up to take Chelsea's seventh penalty. If he scored, I was due up next and my legs had already gone to jelly. I signalled to Edwin to go left. Luckily, he ignored me and went right. And saved it! We tore down the pitch (left) towards the big man, our hero. We'd won the Champions League, the biggest club prize of them all.

"Luckily, Edwin went the right way in the shoot-out and the emotion that followed there... if you could bottle that and sell it you'd be an absolute billionaire."

When you win a massive game like the one in Moscow, especially with the added twist of penalties, it's just an absolute adrenaline rush. Mad. Getting my hands on that trophy – the Big One – and lifting it up alongside Giggsy (right) was as good as it'll get for me as a footballer. Just before I led the team up the steps, Sir Bobby Charlton spoke to me. When an absolute legend of the game praises you, it feels like a dream you don't want to wake up from.

I remember being at the World Cup with England in 2002. We were about to play Brazil: the team of Pelé and Garrincha and all the rest. The kind of game I'd always dreamed about playing in. And, just before the game, I saw my mum and dad and Anton and my mates in the crowd. And I got a bit emotional about it all, to be honest. I choked up a bit. And the game didn't go well. Since then, I've tried to cut emotion out of it when I play. I try to be cold and just focus on what I'm doing. Maybe that means I don't experience and enjoy games in the way that fans do, watching the team. But, after the game in Moscow, it happened again. I was looking round the stadium, trying to take it in a little: had this really happened? Just before we went to pick up the trophy, I saw my mum, charging over the seats to get towards me. And we'd won, another dream come true. The emotion of it all got to me. I think the tears started coming a bit because I remember Vida saying: "Hey, Rio. You can't go and pick up the trophy if you're crying!"

2008/2009

CHAMPIONS OF THE WORLD

Holding the Champions League and Premier League trophies at the same time was something pretty unique. You dream about success as a young player. But your dreams aren't ever this big. And then, when you achieve what you thought was impossible, a weird thing happens. You discover this incredible hunger inside yourself. You want to put down the silverware and just go out and win everything, again and again. After the success of 2007/2008, nothing felt impossible or unwinnable.

Games	(Subs)	Goals	Yellow	Red
43	(0)	0	3	0

Final league position: 1st

Champions League finish: Finalist

Main honours: Premier League title winner; UEFA; FIFA Club World Cup winner; League Cup winner; Community Shield winner; PFA Team of the Year.

Manchester United versus Portsmouth? An ordinary game. But not when you play it in Nigeria in late July (above). We'd been in South Africa for the Vodafone Challenge and fitted in a dress rehearsal for the Community Shield – in the capital, Abuja – on the way home. Before that, the trip to Johannesburg was great: we played Orlando Pirates and Kaiser Chiefs and I swapped shirts with Pirates' Lucas Thwala after we'd beaten them 1–0 in Soweto (left). It was inspiring: football's huge in South Africa, the people's game. Anyone who went to the 2010 World Cup, or watched it on TV, will know how passionate and welcoming the fans in South Africa can be.

"The rise of African football is great for the game. The national teams have made an impact at world cups and African players are making an impact everywhere at club level. People can be inspired by that and seize their own opportunities."

"Being in that kind of company was great.
But we should have had more players in those
team selections over those couple of years."

That's Gordon Taylor (below), head of the Professional Footballers'
Association (PFA) presenting me with an award for making the World
Team of the Year. It was a great honour to be alongside players such as
Messi, Kaka, Xavi and Ronny, who won World Player of the Year (right).
But to be honest, we were the best team in the world at that time and
I don't think it was reflected in those team picks. Ronny deserved his
award, though. It would be great to see him back at Old Trafford again.

To be honest, I would take Ronny as maybe being the best player in the world. Lionel Messi's phenomenal, but he has the Barça team set up to get the best out of him and he's got two of the greatest midfielders anywhere – Xavi and Iniesta – playing in behind him. I think Ronny could go to any club and – however they set up, however good or not they are – he'll still score goals for them. You could put him straight into any team in the world. He'll do things for you on his own.

As champions of Europe, we were invited to play in
the FIFA Club World Cup. That meant another trip east
(below). We played the Japanese side Gamba Osaka in
our semi-final and it turned into a bit of a classic: we
were 2–0 up at half-time and ended up winning it 5–3.
We were down to ten men in the final but Wayne's goal
saw off LDU Quito of Ecuador, and we became the first
English team ever to win the competition (right).

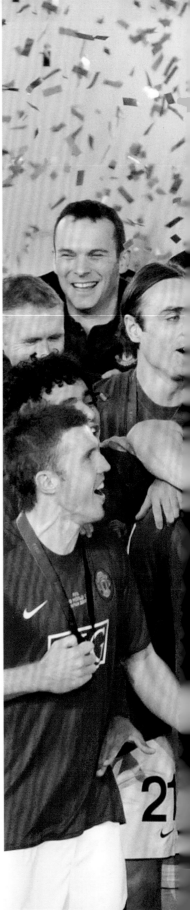

"I was captain when we won the Club
World Cup. Amazing! We're still the
only English team that's ever been
able to say we're world champions."

The new Champions League campaign was a bit like hard work. Got lively once or twice, too: Wazza had to step in and calm things down against Aalborg in Denmark (above). We made it through the group, though, and then drew Inter Milan. They had plenty of big names: Balotelli, Ibrahimović, Stanković and the Brazilian, Adriano (right), who I'd played against for England in the past. We should have won in the San Siro but drew 0–0. Beat them 2–0 at Old Trafford, though, and then knocked Porto out in the quarters. We had a trophy to defend, didn't we?

A pat on the back from the boss (left) and a big grin off Jonny Evans
(above) who played alongside me at Wembley that day. We battered Spurs
in the Carling Cup Final – 20-odd shots on goal, I think it was – but it went
to extra time and pens. Ben Foster had made a great save from Aaron
Lennon in normal time and then saved Spurs' first penalty in the shoot-out.
He won Man of the Match and we won the cup. Happy days.

I'll tell you: it's a long walk back to the centre circle (left). I'd just missed a penalty in the shoot-out against Everton in the FA Cup semi-final. We beat Southampton, Spurs, Derby and Fulham on the way to Wembley and were the better team on the day, I thought. We won our one-on-ones, anyway, like me up against Tim Cahill (above), but didn't make enough chances. And then a former United keeper, Tim Howard, saved Dimitar Berbatov's spot-kick as well as mine. Out. And it hurt. Our chances of an unprecedented quadruple (of League and FA Cups, Premier and Champions' Leagues) had gone.

The Three Amigos (from left: Vida, Edwin and me) celebrate with another Premier League trophy after a draw against Arsenal had put us clear of the pack. It was United's 18th championship, putting us level with Liverpool, as well as our third in a row. From the moment we started playing together regularly, it clicked for me and Vida. It just worked, without us having to say much or even do a lot together in training. We understood each other's games and dovetailed really well. Twenty-four clean sheets that season was something for us – and the goalie – to be proud of.

"Vida likes to attack the ball. I like to get round and clean up. Perfect partnership."

The Champions League Final was at the Stadio Olimpico in Rome. We beat Arsenal in the semis and became the first holders since Juventus in '97 to make the final the following year. Barcelona were fantastic going forward, though, with Lionel Messi, Samuel Eto'o and Thierry Henry (above). And we struggled a bit on the night as they won 2–0. Watching them pick up the trophy – our trophy! – was a horrible moment (right). But I think you learn more about yourself in defeat. That's how I've been throughout my career: I try to analyse what went wrong and come back a better player.

2009/2010

STOP AND START

Eighteen league titles. One more would beat Liverpool's record; would put our names in the history books and a smile on the face of every Red. We were motivated alright. And I wanted to be in the thick of it. But my season was disrupted by a series of injuries which meant I never settled into any kind of rhythm. Just 20 or so appearances tells its own story. Frustrating, even though there were still some highs to enjoy.

Games	(Subs)	Goals	Yellow	Red
21	(1)	0	0	0

Final league position: 2nd

Champions League finish: Quarter-finalist

Main honours: League Cup winner

"My ideal five-a-side team, out of the current squad, would be me at the back, Robin and Wazza up front, Scholesy and Carrick in midfield... or maybe Scholesy and Giggsy."

Nani and me are playing Futsal (left), FIFA's version of five-a-side. We're in Malaysia's capital city, Kuala Lumpur — check out the amazing view! We went on tour to Malaysia, Indonesia and South Korea this pre-season, and we trained in Seoul's World Cup Stadium (above) a day before playing FC Seoul. I like a bit of five-a-side in training. Keeps you sharp, and if you could film our sessions at United you'd be surprised at how intense they can be, with players screaming at others when they make mistakes. Actually, I'm often the player doing the screaming.

Usher is a great singer. I was thrilled to meet him in 2008 to do an interview. It's good for me because it takes me out of my comfort zone and it takes me out of football for a bit. Sometimes, it can get too intense and you can get too wrapped up in it. It's definitely one of the benefits of being a famous footballer, the way doors open and you get a chance to meet your heroes and other interesting people you admire. A couple of years later, I took Nani to the Manchester Evening News Arena to see Usher play. He was outstanding.

Maradona was my childhood idol. Carlos Tevez knew him back in Argentina, and when he turned up at our training ground, I was made up. I wasn't the only one. Training pretty much stopped. We were all flocking around him like little kids. I kept on saying to Carlos, make sure I get a picture with him. That picture is actually hanging up in my changing room locker.

"Getting to meet these people, people I would pay to go and

Scan this page to see
Rio meet with music
A-listers

Carlos Tevez was a great player for us and I'd never have a bad word to say about him. But it was weird him lining up against us for City, especially after some of the things that City had said and done after the transfer. I've always had this feeling that maybe Carlos didn't really want to leave Old Trafford. But things happened and he's his own man and you have to respect his decisions. That's not the kind of move, though – United to City – that I can imagine making. But he was a top player at United. He was always hanging out with Patrice Evra and Park Ji-Sung. That's a Frenchman, an Argentinian and a South Korean: I'm still not sure how they got on so well, but they did!

It was voted the best game of the first twenty years of the Premier League: September 20, 2009, Old Trafford. United v City. With the extra spice – if it needed any! – of Carlos Tevez (left) lining up in a blue shirt. We took the lead three times. Each time, City equalised. And then Michael Owen came off the bench and got the winner six minutes into injury time. We just never give it up! A month later, we beat Bolton 2–1 (above) and made it seven wins from the first nine games.

We played three teams in the Champions League that we'd never
faced before: Besiktas, CSKA Moscow and Wolfsburg, who had
Edin Dzeko (left) playing up top. We only lost one game in the
group (away in Turkey) but some of the others were pretty close.
We needed a goal from Giggsy (above) to help us beat Wolfsburg
at Old Trafford. I've said it before: the bloke's a phenomenon.
The way Ryan's adapted his game over the years: after starting
out at United in the early '90s as a tricky winger, all left foot,
he can now play all over the park. No wonder he's one of the
most respected players in world football.

We do love a comeback at United. In the semi-final of the Carling Cup, City beat us 2–1 at their place. We fancied it at Old Trafford, though, and got it back to 3–3 on aggregate. In injury time – when other teams might have been waiting for extra time – Wayne got the winner with a header from the edge of the six-yard box. Old Trafford went mad. So did we, later on (right). That was the only Carling Cup game I played all season and a back problem kept me out of the final. I was just another Red at Wembley, cheering the boys on against Villa as we picked up our first trophy of the season.

"It's about being mentally strong. We're never out of a game until the final whistle."

We drew AC Milan in the last 16 of the Champions League and did the hard work at the San Siro, winning 3–2. At Old Trafford, it was just about finishing the job. We beat a team that included Andrea Pirlo, David Beckham and Ronaldinho (left) 4–0: two more for Wayne and one each for a couple of unsung United heroes, Park Ji-Sung and Darren Fletcher. Next round, though, Bayern Munich put us out. Even though we won 3–2 at Old Trafford, they went through on away goals.

"Becks played for Milan that night, the first time he'd played at Old Trafford since leaving for Real Madrid. He said it felt like coming home. That's what the place does to you."

Not exactly the catwalk (left): trying on the new season's home kit. I remember being like a little kid when I signed for United. The kit was like a Christmas present I couldn't wait to get into. How did it look? How did it feel? Did it fit? Then, after a decade away from Upton Park, it felt a bit strange running out for a game in West Ham colours (right) but I was never going to miss this chance. The occasion was a testimonial for Hammers' youth team coach Tony Carr. Thirty-five years at the club and a big, big influence on me and generations of Academy players at West Ham. Tony and his staff – guys like Paul Heffer – were fantastic. They taught us all such good habits. I can still remember me and Frank Lampard staying behind after training to work on our technique. Tony pushed us – and we learnt to push ourselves – to become better footballers.

"When I arrived at United, the kits didn't do us players any favours. Baggy? Well, I'm an XL. It looked like I was wearing XXXL. Gary Nev's was even worse: he looked about four foot tall in his."

ROAD TO WEMBLEY

2010/2011

It wasn't the best summer I've ever had. Injuries kept me out of the World Cup in South Africa and I missed pre-season and the start of the new Premier League campaign. It's hard being patient but I was back in September, desperate – like we all were – to get the title back off Chelsea. And there was more: the Champions League Final was going to be played at Wembley. I was already dreaming about winning the thing at the home of English football.

Games	(Subs)	Goals	Yellow	Red
29	(0)	0	0	0

Final league position: 1st

Champions League finish: Finalist

Main honours: Premier League title winner;
Community Shield winner.

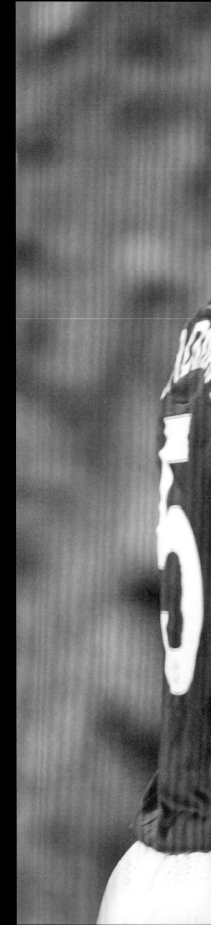

My first game back from injury was against
Rangers at Old Trafford in the Champions
League. I felt good although (above) I was
worried about Wayne after he turned over an
ankle. And much worse followed when Antonio
Valencia broke his leg really badly. You're just
sick for a team-mate when that happens. We
pushed on, though, in our next group game,
away to Valencia, and Javier Hernández got
the only goal (right) just a few minutes after
coming off the bench. Chicharitooo!

I love a tackle, me! Fernando Torres doesn't look so sure, though (right), during our Third Round FA Cup win over Liverpool: I just never get tired of beating them. We didn't lose a game in the league until February and took that confidence on into the Cup. We knocked out Southampton, Crawley and Arsenal, too, on the way to the semi-final. A few days before we faced Manchester City at Wembley, I got my best suit on (above) for the Children's Champion Awards at the Grosvenor House Hotel in London. I don't like to dwell too much on that Wembley semi, a game we sadly lost 1–0.

All smiles for the media from myself and the manager (right). Sir Alex and I were taking questions ahead of our Champions League quarter-final second leg against Chelsea. You probably had to be part of United to understand what the boss is really like as a person. He's got incredible charisma and he's got a proper sense of humour, too. If we were travelling, he'd be the first to have a laugh about what someone was wearing or doing. He'd have a joke with us on the training ground as well but when it was time to work, that was it: he demanded complete focus, 100 per cent effort and all your desire. Those were his exact qualities as a manager, of course. Sir Alex is the number one reason why United are the most successful club in the country.

"How Raúl never won European Player of the Year at least once playing for Real Madrid, I'll never know."

After beating Marseilles and Chelsea in the Champions League knockout rounds, we drew Schalke 04 in the semis. I can't remember what the boss was telling me in training before the first leg (above, left). But I wouldn't be surprised if we were discussing Raúl (right), one of my toughest ever opponents when he was playing for Real before the move to Schalke. Giggsy and Wayne (above, right) scored out in Germany and then we beat them 4–1 at Old Trafford. Which meant Wembley and our third Champions League Final in four years.

Suited and booted by Paul Smith outside Carrington ahead of the Champions League Final: sharp grey mohair and wool whistles, white shirts and – of course – red silk ties. Most of the lads come and go in tracksuits but it's important to look professional at the right time. We're United, after all. This shot was part of the build-up, ten days before Wembley, but we all knew we still had our last league game of the season to play before the final.

"My dad was involved in making clothes and I used to love it
as a kid, looking at all that stuff – the fashions, fabrics, designs.
Inspired me to do a bit of that myself."

The biggest game of the run-in was our home match against Chelsea in May (above).
We needed to bounce back after losing at Arsenal and we turned in one of our best
performances of the season. Chicharito scored inside the first minute – which made
a change from us scoring a minute from the end! – and then Vida added a second
before half-time. They were better in the second half and Frank Lampard scored, but
we held on. And then we won the title with a draw at Blackburn a week later. That
meant we were able to celebrate with the fans at Old Trafford (right) after our
last game of the season, a 4–2 win over Blackpool.

"We'll take any chance for a laugh we can get. But this squad knows how to take training seriously, too."

Someone's been mugged off! Wayne and I are having a laugh before the final against Barcelona. It was probably a practical joke. And it probably involved someone's phone. To be honest, though, training at Carrington is something we take very seriously: the focus and the concentration you need to prepare for big games. Before a Champions League final, the atmosphere's always going to be a bit more intense: the media and the fans are all over it. But the training's at the same high level as ever. The gaffer wouldn't have it any other way.

"We didn't do ourselves justice against Barcelona, in 2009 or 2011. They did a job on us and of course they had the little man, Messi, who was the big difference in both games."

We prepared really well for the Champions League Final and we weren't stupid enough to imagine it being at Wembley would give us any kind of home advantage. We'd worked on cutting down the space Barça had, restricting the angles they needed for their pattern of play, and we started the game really well. But they found their rhythm and the little 10 – Messi – got himself on the ball. Barcelona are about as tough an opponent as I've ever faced in Europe. I respect them but that didn't make watching them celebrate a 3–1 win at Wembley any easier to swallow.

Lionel Messi is the most elusive player I've ever played against. He's a striker but he doesn't really play up front. Or, at least, he doesn't play right up against the centre-halves. In the two finals against Barcelona, he'd drop deep: half the time, me and Vida were closer to each other than we were to Messi. And then, if you follow him into midfield, one of their other players can get in behind you. He takes you places where, as a defender, you don't really want to be and then, when he gets his chance – for a goal or a pass – he's clinical. And so are the rest of that team.

It didn't make up for Wembley a couple of days before but it took our minds off it for a few hours. Our open-top bus tour started at Manchester Cathedral. On a Number 19 – to mark the 19th league title – we edged through the city, down Chester Road and past Old Trafford. It was an incredible spectacle: I've got no idea how many thousands of Reds turned out in the rain to wave us into the history books. I love the Premier League trophy: it's that heavy you need both hands to get it up over your head. I should know: at United we get plenty of practice, don't we?

Scan this page to see Rio's video from on top of the Parade Bus

"Thinking back over my career, the big games that we've lost are the ones that have stayed with me the longest."

The thing about both those finals was that we were beaten well before the final whistle. A couple of goals down and we just couldn't see how to get ourselves back into either game. We didn't do ourselves justice and were well beaten both times, almost as if we'd set them up to be talked about as the best team in the world. And, even though we'd won the league, that defeat just ruined the summer. I remember before one of the open-top bus parades: we were all sitting around, long faces; you'd have thought we'd lost the title not won it. But we were all still thinking about losing to Barcelona. The manager had to pick us up: 'It's a great achievement. You've won the hardest league in the world. You should go out and celebrate it properly with the fans.'

2011/2012

THE NOISY NEIGHBOURS

In the blue half of Manchester, they were buying big: Samir Nasri, Sergio Agüero and the rest. At United, midway through the season, we were welcoming back Paul Scholes, one of the most naturally gifted players in the world. It said it all about Scholesy that he could come back after six months 'in retirement' and straightaway be competing with the best in training. His passing was radar-like and made him the best dictator of a game that I've ever played alongside. And he always had a goal in him, too. Having him back was great for all of us.

Games	(Subs)	Goals	Yellow	Red
29	(0)	0	0	0

Final league position: 2nd
Champions League finish: Group stage
Main honours: Community Shield winner

Back a bit, back a bit...! Just as well I've got a head for heights: we're on top of the Space Needle in Seattle for a coin-toss staged for the US media (left). Me, Vida, the ref and the Seattle Sounders captain, Kasey Keller. Back at ground level, as part of a 5 game pre-season tour, we beat the home team 7–0. A week later, on the other side of the country, we turned up at the White House (above). The President wasn't at home but we were given the tour. I took some photos, but when I put them up on Twitter, it all turned into an episode of '24' and Homeland Security made me take some of them down.

While we were in the US, I took part in a fans' web chat (above). And schooled Nani at table tennis (left). Destroyed him; in front of the cameras, too. There's been some competition down the years: Robin van Persie's pretty good. Cristiano was as well. But I'm the man. I grew up playing table tennis at our youth club. Love the game. I used to bury Michael Owen while we were on England duty. Mind you, he'd always get his own back on the pool table.

Why always him? Mario Balotelli and me on a collision course in the 2011 Community Shield at Wembley. City were 2–0 up at half-time but we never felt out of the game. Chris Smalling got us a goal back and then Nani scored an equaliser with half an hour still to go. Then he scored the winner as well, way into injury time. That comeback set us up for a really good start to the season: we smashed Arsenal 8–2 at Old Trafford early on. I hadn't been involved in a scoreline like that since schoolboy football. Couple of weeks later, though, we were on the wrong end of one when Balotelli and his mates came to Old Trafford and did us 6–1. And there was worse to come from City the following May.

"We weren't used to being challenged by our sky-blue neighbours. It was a new experience…"

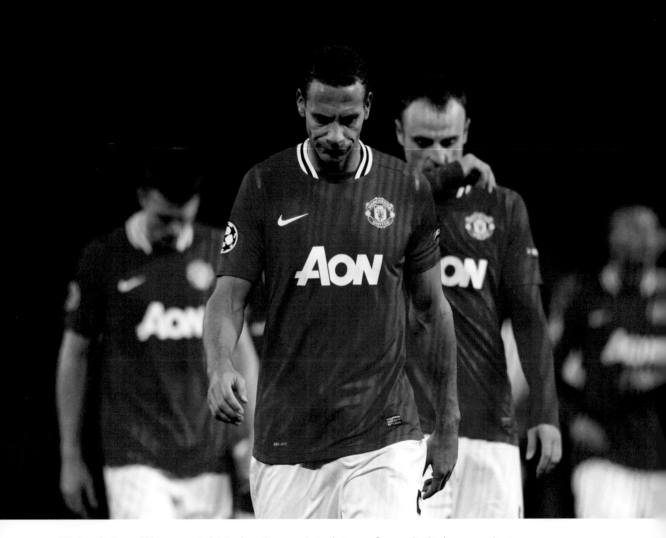

We're fed up. We were right to be disappointed, too, after a 2–2 draw against Benfica at Old Trafford. We never really hit our stride in that season's Champions League: we drew away to Benfica and then at home to Basel before beating the Romanian champions, Otelul Galati, twice. It was in our own hands at home to the Portuguese – a win would have seen us through to the knockout stages – but we came up short and had to travel to Switzerland still needing a result.

Getting to grips with FC Basel striker Marco Streller during a game we let slip away. A point would have seen us through, but Streller scored early on and then Alexander Frei got another in the second half. In between, Vida had to go off with a knee injury and, even though Phil Jones scored with a header, we couldn't find a comeback. Relegated to the Europa League, we beat Ajax but then went out to an excellent Athletic Bilbao side. Wasn't our season in the cups: we went out early in the League and FA cups as well.

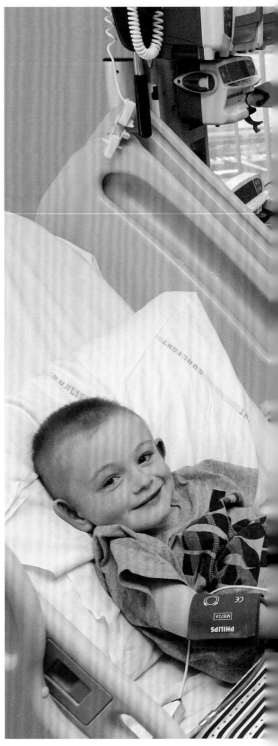

The kids are incredible. And the staff are, too. It's a privilege going onto children's wards at Christmas time, carrying on a United tradition, not least because I'm a dad myself. Here's me with Taylor (above) at the Royal Manchester Children's Hospital. And with Mame Biram Diouf at the bedside of McKenzie (right): he's eight years old and the boy knows his socks! We take in presents for the kids and iPads for the wards. And we get smiles like McKenzie's in return. It's humbling in the best possible way.

By the time Liverpool – and Luis Suarez (left) – came to Old Trafford in February, we were flying, in the middle of a 12-game unbeaten run. Like I say, I never get tired of winning against them and it finished 2–1. Wazza got both goals that afternoon. He got the first away to Tottenham, as well, while I had my hands full with Emmanuel Adebayor (above). White Hart Lane's one of my favourite grounds: great pitch, old-fashioned stadium with the supporters right on top of you. And there's always an atmosphere. Like any ground, though, the best bit is winning there. So we did, 3–1.

More ping-pong (can't get enough of it), but this time for a really good cause. Wayne and I are at the United training ground in March 2012, the day after a league win over West Brom. There, we entertained kids from a school in Preston who'd raised a stack of cash for Sport Relief. The charity made over £67 million in 2012. Phenomenal. I was reluctant to put on the headband at first, but Wayne got straight in there, so I had to join in. Wazza's not bad on the table actually. The kids were split into two teams. Needless to say, Team Rio did a number on Wazza's outfit, did them completely. Blew them off the table.

Scan this page to see something worthy of COMIC Relief

Last game of the season, away to Sunderland. We've won. But we're in a complete state of shock. The last minute of the whole campaign killed us. When the final whistle went at the Stadium of Light, we were champions. But then the news came through from City. My brother was playing for QPR at the Etihad and, despite being down to ten men, they were 2–1 up going into injury time. You know what happened next: two late goals and City took the league. There was devastation in our dressing room: the disappointment, the total disbelief. How had that happened?

"In the dressing room at the Stadium of Light, the boss said: 'Remember the feeling. Remember their fans laughing at you, chanting, happy that you lost. Take that feeling into next season.' We did."

2012/2013

RETURN OF THE REDS

Coming second's horrible. You lie awake trying to work out what went wrong. But it can drive you on, too. Good players – good teams – learn from failure and come out stronger. From the first minute of pre-season, you could see the extra focus, the extra desire in everybody. We were serious about getting the title back. Training was as intense as I can ever remember and the new lads, Shinji Kagawa and Robin van Persie, were part of that straightaway.

Games	(Subs)	Goals	Yellow	Red
34	(3)	1	3	0

Final league position: 1st

Champions League finish: Round of 16

Main honours: Premier League title winner; PFA Team of the Year.

We visited three continents that pre-season, playing in Germany, Sweden and Norway after travelling first to South Africa (launching the new white away kit, above) and then to China (left), where I sign some autographs after arriving in Shanghai. I try to keep in contact with fans when I can. It's actually why I joined Twitter in the first place, to get closer to fans and to get myself across, let them have more access to my thoughts and opinions. I thought, if I was a young kid, I would love to have that, a bit more access and contact with someone I look up to. I now have over four million followers on Twitter. Unbelievable.

"Like I said on Twitter at the time, the worst part
of it was that it was only a two-pence piece.
Could have chucked me a quid, at least!"

The Manchester derby at the Etihad in December was a lively one. A
great game that Robin won with a free kick right at the end. But there
was the other stuff, too. A pitch invader got after Joe Hart and I got
hit by a coin (above) whilst celebrating the winner in front of our fans.
Not in front of City's like some people reported it. Anyway, it got me
just above the eye: you can see where as me and Ashley Young
celebrate after the game (right). Not that I was worrying by then: our
supporters were made-up beating City, and victory put us six points
clear in the league. For all sorts of reasons, I loved winning that game.

Standing between Jonny Evans and Shinji Kagawa as we line up at the Bernabéu in Madrid (above). Some people feared for us when we drew Real in the first knockout round of the Champions League. Me? I couldn't wait. I'm in football for games like these. We played well in Spain and I love the picture (right) of me steering the ball away from Gonzalo Higuaín after we'd broken up one of their attacks. No idea what Ronny's smiling about but he did score with a fantastic header for their equaliser after Danny Welbeck gave us the lead. Getting a 1–1 out there felt like a good result. Everyone was looking forward to getting them back to Old Trafford.

Scan this page
to hear Welbeck
speak about Rio

"We had huge belief all season in our ability to overcome any setback. Big, big confidence."

Getting touch-tight to a quality player I know all about. The second leg against Real was Cristiano's first game at Old Trafford since £80 million had prised him away in 2009. The stadium was absolutely rocking that night: as good an atmosphere as I can ever remember. We were 1–0 up and going through until the ref gave Nani a straight red for an unintentional foot up on Arbeloa. It was a joke: ruined the game and our chances of winning it. I clapped the ref off at the end because his one terrible decision had decided the game. Maybe that wasn't the best thing to do, the right thing to do. But the importance of the game and all the emotion that came with that meant I lost myself for those few moments after the final whistle.

Between mid-November and early April, we went 18 league games unbeaten. And we won 16 of those. At the end of February, we won 2–0 at QPR thanks to goals from Rafael (above, left) and Giggsy. That put us 15 points clear at the top of the table. They were all chasing us from there. Even though the headline writers would have you think different, there's never one single game that decides a season. We had so many moments that turned the tide for us: Robin's hat-trick at Southampton, coming from 2–0 down at Villa to win 3–2, and winning 4–3 at Newcastle after being behind three times.

Scan this page to hear
Robin van Persie
talk about Rio

We could have gone out of the FA Cup at the first time of asking, away to West Ham in Round 3. But Robin's equaliser saved us and we beat them at Old Trafford, and then knocked out Fulham and Reading before drawing Chelsea in the quarter-finals. They'd knocked us out of the League Cup, 5–4, and then we'd beaten them 3–2 in the league, so everyone was expecting something special. We let go of a 2–0 lead at Old Trafford, though, and then lost to a Demba Ba goal at the Bridge. The handshake with Ryan Bertrand (above) was the decent thing, but my face (right) tells the real story. Another chance gone.

"I've won almost everything at United – all the big prizes – but I'm still desperate to get to Wembley and win an FA Cup Final."

This is what winning looks like. And feels like. We got our title back from City with four games left to play thanks to Robin van Persie's first-half hat-trick at home to Aston Villa. His second goal that night, an incredible volley, was pure class. Summed up his season: he made a huge difference for us up front. Twenty-six league goals tell their own story. I played my part too: with not too many injury problems, I think I was pretty solid and consistent. Four of us – me, RVP, Michael Carrick and David de Gea – were named in the PFA Team of the Season.

Scan this page to see
celebration footage
from MUTV

"Sir Alex announced his retirement a few days
before the game and that goal felt like the perfect
way to say 'thanks and goodbye' to a great man."

Swansea at Old Trafford, May 12, 2013. Just
before the celebrations started: my first United goal
for five years (above). It hit the back of the net so
hard it actually lifted the goal off the ground.
I was so chuffed my sons could see me score,
now they're old enough to know and understand
football. And it was a perfect way to say thanks to
the greatest, the gaffer (right) Sir Alex. Stretford
End, last few moments of a game: it had him written
all over it. That never-say-die, attacking attitude he
inspired in all of us. We all owe him a lot.

My turn to MC as we parade another Premier League trophy in Manchester. That's 20 up for United. I'd always thought my first league title would stay as my favourite but, maybe because of the year before – and people writing me off, saying I was finished, that injuries had washed me up – this one might turn out to be the sweetest of the lot. For us all to come through and prove so many people wrong was so satisfying. And then the season finished with a ridiculous 5–5 against West Brom at The Hawthorns. Well, the gaffer's 1,500th and final game was never going to be a dull one, was it?

"We only drew the last game, so the gaffer got the chance to tell us what he thought of us in the dressing room one last time. Only this time he was able to do it with a smile on his face."

RIO FERDINAND

OFF THE PITCH

Being a professional footballer can be a bit like living in a bubble sometimes: all pressure. You need a life away from the game to keep a balance, I think. Being a well-known sportsman has definitely opened some doors for me: I've met living legends and personal heroes from music, film, fashion and other sports. And I've been able to use my profile in other ways too: raising money, raising awareness for causes I believe in; giving something back and helping out where I can.

Getting the message from a couple of schoolchildren from Flixton in Manchester while we were opening a new playground there. I love being with kids: if I hadn't been a player, I'd have ended up as a youth worker somewhere, I think. I recently set up the Rio Ferdinand Foundation, helping young people towards training and qualifications and, after that, a decent career. Not everyone's going to be a pro footballer or a singer or an actor. But there are lots of other jobs in those fields that you can guide kids towards. You want to help make a future possible.

244

帥

氣

雨堯

Myself and Anders Lindegaard looking sharp – but maybe not as sharp as the little fella with us – at a charity fashion show in China, in aid of The Manchester United Foundation. Fashion's always fascinated me – I inherited that from Dad – and it's been great being able to bring out my own range of #5 clothing and accessories. The world of fashion can take me right out of my comfort zone though. I remember a Fashion Relief show I did with Naomi Campbell, surrounded by supermodels, men and women. I found myself feeling like the ugly kid! But the fact that the night was raising money for a good cause made me just swallow hard and get on with it.

In 2011, I interviewed Pele for #5, my online lifestyle magazine. I was nervous – properly nervous, like a kid – going to meet him: a complete legend, one of my childhood heroes, someone I'd been watching videos of all my life. And there he was: a great guy, incredibly friendly. I'll treasure that time with him, listening to him talk about his experiences and giving his views on modern football. I gave him a United shirt with his name on (above). It just left me imagining what it might have been like to play alongside him.

"Meeting Pele and him actually recognising me as I walked in the door was unreal. It was: Wow! This is the Great Man. How does he know who I am?"

Scan this page to
see Rio meet Pele

"The good thing is that you notice that these guys are just normal people once you meet them. They're just built up in the media to be superstars. But they're normal people – just very, very talented."

Ever since we started #5 as a free digital lifestyle magazine, we've tried to include interviews with serious A-listers in each issue. That's the Wimbledon men's singles trophy and holding it is the brilliant Roger Federer. What a talent. I like tennis and play occasionally, but nothing top drawer. This was one of my favourite interviews, seeing as he's one of my heroes. To get to meet Roger at his house next to Wimbledon after he'd won yet another title there was extraordinary. His initials, RF, match mine. What can I say, we've been blessed!

I would have loved to have been a singer but if it's not to be, then the next best thing is getting to know some of the world's top musicians and performers. For #5 I got together with Rita Ora (left), a great girl, great singer and brilliant interviewee. #5 magazine has also allowed me to pursue my interest in fashion and the magazine now has its own on-line store. The distinctive urban look of our gear is shown here (below left) by our four fashionistas.

Scan this page to see #5 magazine's top A-lister interviews by Rio.

"Meeting 50 Cent and talking to him – really talking, not just about him as an artist but about him as a businessman – was absolutely fascinating."

For the mag, the superb 50 Cent (below, left) talked to me about business, politics and his feelings about the USA. He's an intriguing man, a real thinker. And he was on the cover of our first issue, too. One Direction's Harry Styles (below, right) owns a United shirt with my name and number on it. Top man! He even wore it on stage when I turned up to see him at Manchester's MEN Arena in March 2013. So I returned the compliment by giving him a bit of a post-gig nosh-up at my restaurant – plus a VIP ticket to see us play Reading. It's all about who you know!

Scan this page to see Rio meeting with One Direction's Harry Styles.

Me and Damon Albarn are just mucking around while the photographer's trying to get a shot for the cover of issue 10. Damon's a very funny guy and I liked him a lot. Apart from the fact that he's a big Chelsea fan, obviously. It's the people who've agreed to be interviewed who've helped make #5 such a success. I was very proud when it won Apple's 'Best Newsstand App' award in 2011.

Fans mean so much to me. I look back to when I was a kid, I wanted to be as close to footballers as I could. I used to buy magazines every week, and videos. That's why I love going on social media – it's an opportunity to engage with fans. I want the supporters to be able to get closer to me and my team-mates and that is why it was important for me to include them in this book.

Through social media I have been able to reach out and find my ultimate fan. Jamel is 17 years old, lives in Ashford in Kent, and is a lifelong Manchester United fan. He plays centre back for his school The Archbishop's School Canterbury.

"My three words to describe Rio are hard working, inspiring and dedicated"

Jamel McFarlane

Scan this page to see Rio interview his Ultimate Fan Jamel.

OLD
TRAFFORD
TESTIMONIAL

Old Trafford has grown and developed since I first came here, but the thrill of running out onto that pitch never leaves you. By giving me a testimonial match, the club has honoured me for my services to Manchester United. But for me... I just feel privileged. It's an honour, really, to have been asked to stay at this place for that many years. I didn't expect myself to be here for a full decade when I walked through that door the first time. So, to be at this stage and this point in my life, and my career, where I can celebrate those ten years is a hell of an achievement. That's what the testimonial means to me. It's a chance to acknowledge all of that and say 'thank you' to everyone watching.

"To be ten or more years at one club, a club as great as United, not many players do that these days. To be able to celebrate that achievement is something I'll cherish, now and always."

Scan this page for exclusive photos, videos and interviews from the testimonial game.

ACKNOWLEDGEMENTS

I would like to thank my mother and father for their ongoing, unconditional support and love throughout my life. My wife Rebecca for working alongside me and supporting me, on and off the field, with everything I do. New Era Global Sports Management Limited for looking after me and being there for the highs and lows. Lastly, the one and only Sir Alex for keeping me on my toes for 10 years.

Bonnier Books would like to thank the following organisations for their assistance in the production of this book: Anorak™ and Red Frog.

PICTURE CREDITS